How to
Become a
Mermaid

"Water is sacred, and mermaids are real! Elyrria Swann captures the true nature of what it means to be in connection with the element of water and the beings that reside within it. Devoid of fluff, this book is made for those truth seekers wanting to develop a deeper relationship with the water within themselves and the world."

SALICROW, AUTHOR OF
THE PATH OF ELEMENTAL WITCHCRAFT

"There is a place we are drawn to for comfort and sanctuary, for it is the place from which we originally came. And there are people with a high level of empathy who are very giving of their love. That place is the water realm, and the people are mermaids, who have come to us in human form to remind us about what we have forgotten. Come and join Elyrria in the mystical undersea world, where you may discover your mermaid or merman within."

TAMARACK SONG,
AUTHOR OF *BECOMING NATURE*

"Elyrria Swann transports us into the magical and ethereal world of water, as she weaves her personal stories beautifully with lessons and techniques designed to develop our own aquatic relationships. She speaks for the water spirits, revealing new dimensions of love, compassion, healing, and well-being. This enchanting book offers us a rewarding and adventurous pathway to balance and harmony with the natural world."

JEAN MARIE HERZEL,
AUTHOR OF *NATURE SPIRIT TAROT*

How to Become a Mermaid

Embodying the Elemental Energy of Water

A Sacred Planet Book

Elyrria Swann

Destiny Books
Rochester, Vermont

Destiny Books
One Park Street
Rochester, Vermont 05767
www.DestinyBooks.com

Destiny Books is a division of Inner Traditions International

Sacred Planet Books are curated by Richard Grossinger, Inner Traditions editorial board member and cofounder and former publisher of North Atlantic Books. The Sacred Planet collection, published under the umbrella of the Inner Traditions family of imprints, is comprised of works on the themes of consciousness, cosmology, alternative medicine, dreams, climate, permaculture, alchemy, shamanic studies, oracles, astrology, crystals, hyperobjects, locutions, and subtle bodies.

Copyright © 2021 by Elle Elyrria Swann

Cataloging-in-Publication Data for this title is available from the Library of Congress

ISBN 978-1-64411-450-6 (print)
ISBN 978-1-64411-451-3 (ebook)

Printed and bound in the United States by Versa Press, Inc.

10 9 8 7 6 5 4 3 2 1

Text design and layout by Virginia Scott Bowman
This book was typeset in Garamond Premier Pro and Futura with Mr Darcy, Analogue, and Corporate used as display typefaces

To send correspondence to the author of this book, mail a first-class letter to the author c/o Inner Traditions • Bear & Company, One Park Street, Rochester, VT 05767, and we will forward the communication, or contact the author directly at **thesedonamermaid@gmail.com**.

Contents

Foreword

William R. Mistele

A man wrote to me and said, "You write about the beauty and magic of water in nature. But when I sit next to the ocean, I feel nothing. The ocean treats me as if I am a desert or a wasteland."

I wrote back and said, "It is the same for me. I am from a line of fathers who were combustion engineers and who sold coal and oil to heat homes. Sensitivity, empathy, and receptivity were never part of their psychological profile. Consequently, for years I had to either meditate on water or write a poem about the sea in order to feel connected."

As a "spiritual anthropologist," I have studied with over fifty masters from many traditions. But none of them had the vibration of water in their auras. After decades of various exercises, I have discovered what works for me. If I meditate on the water content of my blood as it flows through my body, I then feel connected to the water element from within. Whether in my body or in nature, water has the same soothing, purifying, healing, and nurturing qualities. The seas, rivers, and streams now feel part of me, but to arrive at this inner awareness has been a long journey.

Decades ago, and after a great deal of training in the Hermetic tradition of Franz Bardon, I followed his instructions and contacted four mermaid queens on the astral plane. Two of them promised me that I would meet mermaids dwelling in human bodies so I could better understand their race. When I finally understood what they were saying, I placed a global casting call on a modeling website for women who could portray a mermaid on a beach. I received several immediate responses from women who embodied the water element.

My extensive interviews with them led to my posting an essay on the internet called, "Traits of Mermaid Women." Now, about every two months, a woman writes to me from some part of the world. These women often say, "I googled 'mermaid' and 'women' and found your essay. You are the first person to understand who I am. It is like you are inside my head reading my mind."

Elyrria, the author of this book, wrote to me with a similar message. After having spent at least forty hours videotaping my interviews with her, I am currently writing her biography, a novel, and a screenplay based on her life. Her voice is original and authentic. She speaks with the authority that derives from experience.

What are these merwomen like? When you are with one of them, you may notice the following: You feel as if you are out in nature in a place of peace and serenity. You are in geological time, free from the effort of maintaining a social identity. There is no anxiety, insecurity, or fear. You feel safe and caressed—as if you are sitting in a stream and cool, soothing water is flowing over your skin.

And you feel you are with a person who effortlessly gives you 100 percent of her attention. She is completely receptive, responding to you in continuously new ways in each moment. You feel loved and accepted.

It is not that she believes in you. Rather, she sees you as your better self—the person you will be when you have overcome your doubts and conflicts and solved your major problems. Because she possesses a skill known as graphic imagination, she can see and experience your future self as being real right now in this moment.

This does not arise from an act of will on her part. Since she embodies the vibration of water, she does what water itself does: she is endlessly giving, nurturing, calming, and reviving. Just being in her aura makes you feel fully alive. Put simply, in her presence you feel energized and calm, renewed and peaceful at the same time.

What is not taught in our civilization is the essence of the feminine—the accepting grace, the healing power, and the all-embracing love within its magnetic and attractive energy. If our society had the knowledge mermaids do, our empathy would be vastly expanded. Inner kingdoms of feeling would be revealed to us. Our receptivity and sensitivity to impressions and our intuitive abilities would be exponentially increased.

In practical terms, this would mean we would have the ability to understand why others—anyone, anywhere on

Earth—feel as they do. We would be able to perceive and also interact with their souls directly. Such love has the power to hold and contain in our hearts anyone else's life, soul, or will to heal, bring to completion, and transform them from within.

In this book, Elyrria shares a powerful vision—the oceans of the Earth are the outer expression of an inner kingdom of love. This love has no end, and it is inexhaustible. When we find this love, we will no longer perceive nature as external to ourselves. Rather, like her, we will feel united to nature at the core of our being.

WILLIAM R. MISTELE is a spiritual anthropologist and a bardic magician. He graduated from Wheaton College in Illinois in 1969 with a bachelor's degree in philosophy and economics. He later went on to study Hopi culture and language at the University of Arizona, where he received a master's degree in linguistics. He has studied esoteric oral traditions from lineages around the world, including Tibetan Buddhism, Hopi culture, Western Hermetic traditions, and nature religions of Wiccans and Druids, Sufism, Taoism, and Zen. Since 1975 he has been a student of Franz Bardon's teachings on Hermetic magic, a system of training that includes the evocation of and communication with nature spirits. After forty-five years of studying Bardon's system, he has gone on to applying his magical skills to establishing justice between nations. You can find his videos on YouTube, including one in which he, Avaah Blackwell, and Aaron Chledowski interview a number of mermaids and mermen described in Franz Bardon's book, *The Practice of Magical Evocation*. You can find more on his work at williammistele.com. He is the author of several books including *Undines: Lessons from the Realm of Water Spirits; The Four Elements; Mermaid Tales;* and *Mermaids, Sylphs, Gnomes, and Salamanders.*

INTRODUCTION

Meeting Mermaids

During my childhood, I used to comb the shelves at Barnes & Noble looking for books about people who fell in love with fish or who met a mermaid queen in their lucid dreams. I found many books about the folklore and mythology of mermaids, and these were very enjoyable to read. However, they did not satiate my hunger for a practical mermaid guide. I was looking for an owner's manual for mermaids that would tell me how to exist on planet Earth as a mermaid and meet others like myself. But no such book had been written.

While I was growing up, I tried talking to a few people in my small social circle about how much I loved mermaids and how I felt that I was part of their realm. Sometimes a friend would talk about mermaid makeup or dressing up as a mermaid, but mostly I received strange looks and remarks about how weird I was.

Princess Ariel from Disney's *The Little Mermaid* often came up in the conversations, but a large part of me could not buy into this version of mermaids. Fairy tales and mythology were wonderful to hear about, but the subject matter felt alien to the true nature of mermaids. There was always some part of me that intuitively understood that mermaids transcend the ideas of human fashion and literary traditions.

In spite of my conservative upbringing, I always believed in the existence of faeries, merpeople, unicorns, and other mythological beings. As I grew older, I never lost faith in the fact that these creatures exist in a world parallel to ours.

Eventually, I began meeting them.

Mermaids first came to me in visions while I relaxed in the bathtub during my early preteen years. I found that I felt most at home in water and would sometimes spend eight or more hours in the bathtub in my free time. I would often take a good novel with me to read, but it was usually left untouched as I started making contact with real mermaids from the astral mermaid realm, who communicate using empathy and telepathy.

After I was able to see them and feel their presence, I asked them to give me teachers who could help me bring the gifts of the mermaid realm to the people here on Earth. My request was granted. I am here to serve as a channel of information for this beautiful realm and to continue to learn about how to master the water element inside myself.

The mermaid realm holds many treasures, such as empathy, depth of feeling, healing abilities, ecological consciousness, an inner peace with the universe, and unconditional love. In these pages I explain how to cultivate and to bring to full consciousness the archetypal mermaid or merman that exists inside each of us.

CHAPTER 1

What Is a Mermaid?

Mermaids are elemental beings that embody the vibration of water. A simple way to think of it is that they are the personification of the watery element. If water could talk, then it would be a mermaid. The purpose of the mermaid realm is to love and enrich the water element in the spirit world.

Mermaids exist on the astral realm, which, in simple terms, is a spirit realm. It is a place where souls can exist as pure energy without needing a physical body. Beings in the astral realm often retain the physical appearance they had when alive, but they are also free to assume other forms.

On the astral plane, what you think manifests immediately. A general rule is that the more similar you are in vibration to something, the more likely you are to draw it into your life. If you think to yourself, *This will hurt,* you may suddenly feel pain. And if you think, *The pain must go,* then pain will stop. By contrast, on Earth there is a time lag between thought and reality. In the 3rd dimension here on Earth (where we exist in a physical world shaped by linear time), many of us still have negative thoughts or beliefs about ourselves or others. Thought does not instantly become reality here because we have the opportunity to correct misaligned beliefs before they manifest.

The 3rd dimension, where we can make mistakes and learn from them, is the training ground for the 4th dimension, or astral realm. The closer we get to the 4th dimension, the quicker our thoughts become reality.

The astral realm is sometimes referred to as the emotional realm because emotions strongly shape how the world is perceived. The merpeople of the astral realm have mastered their thoughts and emotions to such a degree that they can assist humans with getting in touch with emotions that many of us do not fully understand. Merpeople can also help with the manifestation of dreams, as the astral realm is where people go when they sleep.

Think of the astral realm as a giant space with dozens of doors. One door is labeled "dragons," and another is labeled "faeries," and there are many other magical doors nearby. One of these is a gate leading to the stunning realm of mermaids.

While it is also possible to create one's own mermaid kingdom on the astral plane, creating a mermaid kingdom in the physical world and creating a mermaid kingdom within oneself are good first steps. Doing so can enhance an individual's ability to connect to the mermaid realm. I will discuss the merits of physical interactions with water creatures—both ordinary and as incarnated mermaids—and how they can help us connect to the mermaid realm in chapters 4 and 5.

If you want to interact with mermaids, this will likely involve some internal work for aligning oneself with the vibration of water and the mermaid realm. "Like attracts like" in the astral realm, and mermaids tend to be near the vibrations of things that emulate them. This is why mermaid consciousness is usually easier to sense next to an ocean rather than in the Gobi Desert. Mermaid consciousness is present in any form of water, but it intensifies near larger bodies of water. In other words, if you feel, perceive, and act like a mermaid or merman,* you are more likely to attract their presence. Mermaids generally do not pick and choose whom they associate with as humans do (based on social hierarchy and so on). Like water, they naturally flow to an area of least resistance. Similar vibrations draw them in like two drops of water becoming one.

Mermaids do not live with physical bodies in our ocean; they live in that part of the astral plane that is parallel to our ocean. It is a dimension that exists within the physical water on our planet.

Building mermaid kingdoms works best if you have a good understanding of what water means to humanity. Most of us are aware of our physical need for fluids, but the spiritual integration of water is typically unknown territory. Since mermaids are the energetic ambassadors for the water element, we need to understand the importance of water in our

---

*Mermaids have a signature vibration that is feminine, whereas mermen possess a signature vibration that is masculine. Some beings are a blend of the two energies and do not fit into just one gender or the other. For the sake of simplicity, I more typically use the term *mermaid* in this book. Even though I tend to tune in to the masculine or feminine vibrations, it is important to note that merpeople are gender neutral, and *all* people can communicate and connect with them.

spiritual development. Wearing a mermaid tail, cultivating wavy mermaid hair, and putting on sparkly makeup are fun things to do, but the true spirit of mermaids is independent of physical embellishment. By building a mermaid kingdom inside yourself, you can create your own mermaid realm without ever buying a single fish tank or silicone mermaid tail. Only your inner self and alignment with the watery element can provide access to the beautiful and mysterious world of the mermaids.

CHAPTER 2

The Water Element

Water makes up a large part of our bodies. Adult human bodies are roughly 60 percent water, and infant bodies are composed of an even higher percentage (75 to 78 percent water). Human blood is about 83 percent water. The average human can only survive for about three days without water.

In early pregnancy, amniotic fluid surrounding an infant is mostly made of water. When the amniotic sac ruptures shortly before delivery, this is commonly known as a birthing person's "water breaking." We are born of water and made of it, and yet we know so little about how this affects our emotional, mental, and spiritual bodies. The more we become aware of how water responds to vibrations, the more likely we are to be responsible when it comes to maintaining the energetic aspects of our own physical watery element and the physical bodies of water we share with the people and animals of our world.*

---

*Sadly, it is a privilege to have access to clean drinking water, and while it is important to maintain a healthy water element within you if you are able, it is also important to acknowledge the problem that not everyone has this choice and that those of us who do can also contribute toward the physical and energetic health and abundance of water for all people and animals.

One of my favorite books is called *The Hidden Messages in Water* by Masaru Emoto. In his book, Emoto explained that he exposed water crystals to sounds, words, and energy fields, and then took pictures of the water crystals shortly after imprinting them with those vibrations. He shares those beautiful pictures with the reader.

When the water was exposed to loving music and positive words, it formed beautiful crystals that were whole and stunning. When the water was exposed to negative words or music, the water crystals became malformed and incomplete. Water is receptive and empathic, which means that it responds to vibrations beamed in its direction. Everything in the universe is made of vibrational energy. Negative words carry negative energy, and positive words carry positive energy. The same idea applies to thoughts and intentions that occur in our physical space. If tiny water crystals are sensitive to simple words and phrases, imagine what happens to our bodies when unkind words are spoken near us.

Part of aligning with our highest potential in the mermaid realm is becoming masters of our human vessels and vibrations first. Meditating, chanting, singing, and speaking positively are tools that keep our spiritual and physical bodies aligned. If someone is unable to speak, having positive and healthy thoughts is enough to keep the water element in the body engaged with a positive vibration.

It is also important to make healthy drinking choices. Tap water often has many unhealthy compounds in it in large amounts (such as fluoride, chlorine, arsenic, and perchlorates), and it can quickly throw the body into chaos. Though these things do not always cause disease in small amounts, it is something for the water-conscious human to consider. These are suggestions to help people interested in this topic, but drinking "perfect" water is not necessary to develop spiritually or connect with the mer-realm. Many of us are privileged to live in societies that give us options regarding what we choose to drink, but not everyone is that fortunate. The majority of bottled water is an unhealthy option because the bottles that contain the water are made of thousands of harmful chemicals and potential toxins that negatively affect human health, and it also contributes to plastic waste. The water can become imprinted with these potential toxins and becomes part of us after we drink it.

The best water that we can drink comes from underground aquifers where water is kept cold and dark for extended periods of time. Spring water and artesian water is naturally filtered by the earth and contains important minerals that are not lost in the process of unnatural filtering methods. Freshly gathered spring water should have the same composition and integrity of its source spring.

These are just some ideas to ponder when considering what our regular water consumption habits look like. Not all of these concepts have enough scientific research to warrant terror in the ordinary civilian, and as noted, not everyone has access to all of these choices. The most important part of maintaining integrity with the physical water in our bodies is the vibration we choose to hold and emit.

Purifying our personal space is just as important as choosing healthy drinking water because being near negative people and unconsciously absorbing their vibrations affects us on all levels of our experience. Setting healthy boundaries for ourselves and creating physical spaces that nurture us will work wonders when it comes to consciously connecting to mermaids.

Energy follows the path of least resistance, but it can often be stopped by blockages in our energy system. If we are trying to talk to a mermaid queen after we have engaged in negative self-talk all day, any energy from the mermaid realm is going to be stopped by the physical damage we have inflicted on the water in our bodies, and the mermaid's energy will work toward healing that water. This means that it is less likely that we will have a strong mental or psychic connection to the mermaid realm. There are exceptions to this, of course, but in general, it is important to do our best to be conscious of the vibrations affecting our physical bodies.

The structure of water is simple, but its powers are vast. Water can destroy in the case of tsunamis and tidal waves. It can bring relaxation and healing when it is infused with herbs or bath salts by taking on the physical properties of herbs and medicines that are put into it.. Water is known as the universal solvent, because it can dissolve more substances than any other liquid. Likewise, water can also dissolve as well as integrate feelings, thoughts, intentions, and desires that we put into it. This knowledge opens the door to limitless amounts of psychic and personal potential.

We are all familiar with the role water plays in our everyday lives, but we are perhaps less in touch with the spiritual aspects of water. Visualize a drop of water in your mind. Now, imagine a secondary drop slipping out of the first physical drop. Imagine that the second drop is shimmering and shining softly right next to the first one. This shining drop represents the spiritual water molecule. It is just as real as the physical one and contains incredible potential. Water is receptive, nurturing, and able to mirror thoughts and emotions, as Emoto's work showed the world.

Here is an exercise to help you prepare to integrate the spiritual water element.

Meditation to Integrate the Spiritual Water Element

Place a small cup of water near you or sit next to a stream if one is available to you. You can also choose to sit in a bathtub, which is what I prefer when I do this activity. Sit in a peaceful area in a comfortable position with your palms facing each other. If you choose to sit with your legs crossed, you could maintain the same hand position or rest your hands on your legs with palms open toward the sky.

To set the tone for the meditation, begin to imagine the most uplifting emotion you possibly can. Many people choose the feeling of love because it is a universal experience.

You may want to imagine your lover's embrace, the way you felt when you held your first puppy, the positive flow of good feelings when you taste your favorite food, or how amazing a hug from your mother feels. Picture yourself being fully understood, loved, cared for, and satisfied by this love you are visualizing.

Now, imagine this love as a small, shimmering ball of light (or energy). This energy is emanating from your head and your heart. It is felt by your heart and processed in the brain as imagery. Envision this beautiful energy in your head and heart flowing to your shoulders, down your upper arm, and into your hands.

What does it feel like? Pay attention to every sensation, color, and feeling you experience. Do your arms light up a little bit when the energy passes through? Sometimes even if I do not see anything, I feel a deep sense of relaxation or a slight tingle in the body parts I send loving energy through. Whichever way you experience loving energy is perfect and beautiful.

The important thing is just to maintain the emotion you initially created by visualizing yourself in a loving scenario. Keep visualizing whatever it is that makes you feel this sensation. You can have your eyes open or closed—whatever helps you experience this energy more fully.

When the energy is shimmering within your hands, use your mind to push the energy out between your hands while keeping this feeling of love strong in your emotional body.

I usually open my eyes at this point to look at the

energy between my hands. What you see is your unique signature vibration. My water energy usually looks like a soft, fluid ball of blue-tinted liquid. If the water is pink, diamond-shaped, or shapeless, you are still doing it right. You can even pick an oceanic creature or the image of a mermaid if you like.

This energy you have created is the energy of love. Now, look at the cup of water, the stream, or the bathtub water.

You can place your hands in the water or rest them on the surface, or you can visualize doing so. While keeping the incredible feeling you have conjured at the forefront of your emotional awareness, imagine this energy flowing from between your hands into the water.

If you do not see anything happening physically, use your mind's eye to visualize this energy permeating the water around you as you become one with it. You can even imagine the energy like a bath salt that begins to dissolve in the watery matrix. When you feel that the energy has been blended thoroughly with the water around you, remove your hands and sit back.

Now perceive the water around you. How has it changed? Does it feel more loving or relaxing? Does it feel more "like you"? Does it seem more alive? You have just imprinted the water around you with your signature vibration of love and positive emotion. Now the water is able to respond to you by mirroring this feeling back to you as well as communicating with the water that composes your own physical body.

The meditation you have just learned is one of the valuable treasures that the mermaid realm offers to us. You will use this tool often in your psychic work with mermaid allies, healing work, and personal restoration. Inside my inner mermaid kingdom, I have a box made of pearls and shells where I keep psychic tools and meditations stored. You can visualize this meditation as a key, a shell, a body of water, a shimmering strand of energy, or an image of love.

However you want to visualize it is your choice and is part of your own secret, magical mermaid toolbox. Place this tool gently into your sacred space. It is accessible whenever you want to use it, and you can teach others about this powerful but simple gift from the mer-realm.

〰〰〰〰〰〰〰〰〰〰〰〰〰〰〰〰〰〰〰〰〰

Imbuing water with feelings, emotions, and intentions makes water your ally and gives it even more consciousness. J. R. R. Tolkien wrote that "elves began it, of course, waking trees up and teaching them to speak." This is exactly what we are doing, except it is done with water.

Water is conscious and aware on some level, but because it is so receptive, it is often a blank canvas that we can use to program our desires and dreams for manifestation. You can imprint water with any feeling or emotion that you wish to.

Here are some additional suggestions to help you connect with and make use of the water element.

- Sending positive energy to your water before you drink it has enormous health benefits and begins to create a relationship between you and the mermaid realm.
- Water as a spiritual substance is purifying, receptive, and empathetic. Just visualizing yourself standing under a waterfall of heavenly water programmed with loving energy can completely alter your energy field or aura. All mermaids use psychic energy to program water around them and use it to make the world a better place.
- If a friend of yours is stressed at work, you can create a peaceful, relaxed feeling in yourself and send it to the water in your friend's body. You can also send it to the water in their cup or imagine a sea of loving energy surrounding them until they are more relaxed. Since water is an empathetic entity, it mirrors what we project onto it.
- The possibilities for psychic work with water are endless, and you are allowed to be as creative as you want. Just as water nurtures an infant in the womb, you can create water energies that nurture and give life to everything around you. Plants, people, rocks, animals, and even inanimate objects (such as clothes) can be imprinted with healing water.

If our own vibrational water is pure and of a high frequency, the water inside others begins to mirror ours even when they are not aware of it. This is how mermaids use water when sending healing or positive energy to others. Just knowing about this possibility within the water element automatically brings you into the energy field of the mermaid realm.

All mermaids view water as a living, feeling entity. They use it in most of their healing and psychic adventures, and they have a relationship with it that has become a natural part of who they are.

CHAPTER 3

Incarnated Mermaids and Their Abilities

There are many stories written about mermaids. Some narratives describe how merpeople take on human form and lure sailors to their deaths with their voices. These stories seem to communicate the fear that humans have surrounding the water element. The ocean is very mysterious because we have hardly explored any of it. The same is true for the magical examination of the water element.

Mermaids do occasionally enter our world and live in human bodies. They are born to human families, but their auras are made of water. These mermaids are known as incarnated mermaids. The main reason that merpeople incarnate in human bodies is that they are attempting to connect their realm with the human one. Once in a physical body, by their presence alone merpeople bring together two separate realms.

It is usually obvious from a young age that an incarnated merperson is not entirely human. There are several traits of incarnated mermaids that differ from the average person. The first is that they have an extraordinary amount of empathy.

Many humans have empathy as well but not on the level that mermaids do. Mermaids have so much empathy that they can experience the world from someone else's point of view as if they are living that person's life themselves. They make excellent therapists and counselors because of their ability to literally become another person and know exactly how that person is feeling.

The second trait that mermaids possess is their sense of completeness. Since they are united to a natural element within, mermaids do not need social stimulation the way that most humans do. Mermaids also have no need for social validation. They do not place importance on who likes them and who does not.

Another trait of mermaids is that they are here to love. Mermaid love is not exactly like the human ideas of romance. Mermaids are very giving with their love, so they are able to love more than one person at the same time. But if they gain a romantic partner such as a husband or wife, they will never lose their love for that person, even if they break up or get a divorce.

A mermaid's love is forever, and it is nearly impossible for them to become bitter or resentful no matter how poorly someone treats them. Since mermaids can forgive almost anything, they can have a hard time telling people "no" or getting out of dangerous situations. This can cause some problems for incarnated mermaids. They have to learn how to set boundaries.

Incarnated mermaids have many things to teach us, but because they have different ways of experiencing the world, they can end up as outcasts in our society. I hope to bring more awareness to the existence of mermaids so that this does not happen as often. It does not hurt mermaids emotionally to be rejected by society, but such a scenario is a terrible waste of their gifts and time on the planet.

Mermaids also embody the element of water in unique ways. Some mermaids have auras of waterfalls or mountain pools, each with unique qualities. Almost all of the incarnated mermaid people I know spend incredible amounts of time in water. It helps them feel more at home on our planet. All of them relate to water on a spiritual level and do not understand themselves apart from it. Having an aura made of water means that you do not have the same set of emotional needs as humans. However, merpeople can learn to adopt more of a human personality to help them survive in the human world.

Many incarnated mermaids do not have regular careers because they do not understand the dynamics of a society that "sows seeds and harvests rewards." They tend to go with the flow instead of pursuing an occupation. They do best in relationships where their partner encourages them to create a career centered around their natural talents (such as counselor, artist, or energy healer).

Mermaids have little awareness of time because the astral realm does not have days, weeks, months, or years. It is a neutral space with no constraints on the inhabitants' activities. This can also make it hard for merpeople to hold jobs on Earth. Because of their sense of timelessness, incarnated merfolk often find it hard to keep track of time. This can manifest as being too late, too early, or forgetting about keeping a schedule altogether. Being in physical bodies with limitations can also present a learning curve to newly incarnated merpeople on Earth. Some incarnated merpeople have had enough lives as humans to finally venture onto a career path. Being therapists, counselors, and environmental scientists can help them bring awareness to the importance of empathy and conservation, though they are not limited to these choices. Mermen tend to be more task oriented and devote their energy to keeping ecosystems in balance and making sure that everyone is safe. But there are always exceptions, and merpeople do not limit their tasks or interests based on perceived concepts of gender.

If an astral mermaid or merman tries to get the attention of a human, the communication is rarely successful. Mermaids and mermen communicate on the astral using empathy and telepathy, which few humans have completely mastered.

All incarnated mermaids have some level of psychic ability. Many are born with the ability to see faeries, talk to extraterrestrials, and see energy using their physical eyes. This is because a part of them always remains on the astral plane, and they remain connected with this part of themselves. Some mermaids report that they dream the dreams of dolphins and whales and know when they are in distress. Others have the ability to communicate with these creatures and guide them to safe places telepathically.

Mermaids believe that beauty is something to be appreciated. But beauty to a merperson is different from what beauty is to a human. Incarnated mermaids can definitely notice when someone has nice bone structure or a beautiful face, but beauty to them is centered around the way a person's energy feels. If someone lacks empathy or care for the environment, they do not meet a merperson's definition of beauty.

Even so, merpeople are not unkind to those who are not like them. They love them and seek to bring healing to that person. They can observe when a human feels tired or dead inside, but they approach each situation from a desire to heal what is missing. Mermaids never run out of loving energy, and their empathy usually does not drain them or make them feel tired.

CHAPTER 4

How My Merman Found Me

At the age of four, when I first became aware of myself as someone who felt deeply connected to the water element, I did not even know the word *mermaid* existed. I only knew that I felt connected to the water element in general and felt most at home around fish and creatures that made their homes in the watery realm.

When I was ten years old, beautiful women started coming to me in visions while I was sleeping or in the bathtub. They would call me "sister" and sit in the water with me while sending positive emotions and energy to me through the water element. I had no idea that they were mermaids. I knew that they were magical beings, but at the time I had little education regarding alternate dimensions and planes of existence. I assumed that some of them were spirit guides and only later discovered that they were mermaids from the astral realm.

These mermaid women would usually appear from the waist up, though I occasionally saw that they had legs. When mermaids come to me in visions, they usually have legs.

Mermaids are water, so they are adaptable and can take a form that is slightly more human than their normal physical presentation in their own realm. They are not bound by one singular form.

These women told me that some teachers would be coming to me. They said, "We will come to you in a way that no one will ever suspect. Mermaids and mermen will become your allies by taking physical form and assisting you with your spiritual mission."

At the time, I had no idea what form these beings were going to take, and I was very excited. The mermaids kept appearing to me in the bathtub, and they would take care of me in my sleep like a mother would, but it was several years before I would fully understand the implications of their promise to me.

I spent my first semester in college at a conservative school that I did not want to attend. I had been accepted to other universities that I greatly admired but was sent to a school that reinforced my family's religious background and belief system. I was unhappy, and even before I arrived I was not looking forward to being around people who had completely different passions from mine.

After I arrived at college, I found myself looking for a pick-me-up at the local Barnes & Noble. After listlessly letting my eyes wander over the books for a while, I decided to go into the PetSmart next door to look at the parakeets they had for sale.

I walked in and immediately felt drawn to the back of the store where all of the fish were kept. All of a sudden, it was like something grabbed my sweater and pulled me in the direction of the fish tanks. My brain was shocked that my legs were moving on their own toward this part of the store.

I felt pulled toward the massive tanks of goldfish, koi, and guppies on display and the empty tanks and decorations for sale on the shelves. It was as if my feet were gliding across the floor, and I seemed to reach the fish more quickly than what should have been possible.

After arriving in the fish section, I looked around for a moment until my eyes came to rest on a shelf that was separate from the large display tanks. I felt drawn to a shelf that held little plastic cups. At first I thought the cups just had moss in them, but as I drew closer, I saw that they contained breathtaking betta fish.

My eyes barely had time to scan the cups of fish before I became enraptured with one little fish in particular. There was a slight glow around his cup, and I experienced something similar to tunnel vision, where everything in the background blurred out and the only clear thing I could see was the object I was focusing on.

Instead of flaring or challenging me like betta fish often do to observers, this fish seemed to be performing a small dance for me. He was swimming in adorable circles and inviting me in with his warm, glowing energy. I probably looked weird when I picked up the cup and pressed my nose up against the plastic, but I didn't care. I was not quite sure what was happening, but I intuitively knew that this creature was more than just a fish. His awareness and expression seemed to extend far beyond that of the average fish, and he seemed to have the ability to communicate with emotions. I felt that the joy and excitement within this fish was something that he was trying to use to communicate with me.

I wanted to get back to my dorm room to get to know this fish, so I grabbed some fish food and a plastic bowl, went to the counter, and paid about six dollars for him. It was not until I walked outside into the sunlight that I became aware of the fish's colors. He had a little bit of brown on his chest, but the majority of his scales were a shimmering array of green and blue with a hint of purple in his tail. The label on the cup said that he was a Halfmoon Betta.

I had some obligations to fulfill for the rest of the afternoon, so I left my little fish on my desk in my dorm room after having made sure he was warm and comfortable. Later, when I returned, he entertained me with his tricks and ability to breach like a whale. He would follow my finger endlessly and poke himself out of the surface of the water to lightly tap my fingertips when I hovered them over his bowl. I had never felt any relationship that was this magical before. Human friends were few and far between for me, but even the best of my human relationships were not as loving and playful as the one I had with this fish.

That night I went to sleep with my head at the end of my bed where my feet normally would have been so that I could be a little bit closer to my fish at the end of my desk. I started dreaming almost immediately. One of the stunning women who came to me in the bathtub was present in my dream along with the first merman I had ever seen.

He was everything you would hope for a merman to be,

with muscles, handsome features, and a winning smile. But what I felt when I entered his energy field transcended any physical aesthetic in the human world. His aura was so attentive and loving that I thought, *No human man will ever be able to make me feel the way this being does.*

After a short time of being in the merman's energy field with my mermaid friend waiting nearby, the mermaid said, "We have come to you in another form now. We are here to take care of you and help you fulfill your mission."

The merman stirred slowly and chimed in, "You are observing my astral body right now, but I have come to you in the form of a fish in your world. I am able to take on this temporary shape so that we can be physically near and work on projects together. I cannot stay for long, but I am only one of many, and I will come back to you. We are always with you, and we will always be family."

After they finished speaking, the merman temporarily shapeshifted into the form of the fish I had just purchased, swam in circles around my head, and then returned to his merman form before walking away with the mermaid.

When I jolted awake in my bed, I looked up at the fish on my desk and saw him notice me.

He performed a fancy loop-de-loop twirl in his bowl. It was then that I fully understood what had occurred at the pet store. I had made contact with the mermaid realm, and in its own way, it had come to stay with me in the physical world for a while. Becoming aware of this was the most exhilarating of sensations, and it gave me chills and goose bumps. I realized that a merman had come to me in the form of a fish, and the spirit of the mer-realm was currently dwelling in my bedroom.

I named my fish Dante, and he became my favorite companion. When I was near him, I felt that I was in the mermaid realm. I preferred spending quiet evenings with my fish in my dorm room instead of going to wild parties and social hangouts with the other college students.

I have always been an introvert, but I reached a new level of satisfaction in my personal time that I spent with my fish that even solitude could not give to me. Dante's empathy for me was clear from the start. When I spent a whole day in bed due to a nasty virus, Dante stayed near me with his nose pressed up against the side of his bowl. The next day I was completely better, but Dante was lethargic and struggling to stay upright.

I took him to PetSmart where they tested the water chemistry of his bowl (it was perfect) and tried to figure out what was wrong with him. It suddenly dawned on me while I was standing there in the store: He had energetically taken on a lot of my sickness.

I quickly asked the mermaid realm to help him balance his energy, and the next day he was back to normal. Merpeople in fish bodies will often try to carry burdens that ail their human counterparts, but since their bodies are so much smaller than ours, it can affect them negatively even though they have magical spirits.

Dante only lived with me for about a year before his spirit returned to the mer-realm. I was extremely sad when he passed away, but he came to me in dreams as both a merman and betta fish to let me know that he would keep his promise to come back to me.

In 2014 while I was living at the base of the Rocky Mountains in Colorado, Dante found his way back to me in the form of a new fish. Neptune was a stunning, cerulean Crowntail Betta who was extremely protective of me. Whenever someone would come into my home with negative energy (such as my realtor), he would throw a temper tantrum and flare and swim angrily around his tank until the person left.

Sometimes I would see him using his energy to "push" someone out of the door. Merpeople usually do not get angry in the astral realm, but when they incarnate in fish bodies they can have big tempers. Betta fish are known as Japanese fighting fish for a reason. Neptune made it very clear when he did not like someone, but he was always extremely sweet to me.

Many other fish came to me while I had Dante and Neptune, and they kept coming after my merman left the physical world for the second time. They all had their own particular talents. Sozin (a Red Halfmoon Betta) was very good at letting me know when I needed to go clean up a riverbed near my house. He would enter my dreams and show me locations nearby that had been trashed by tourists/hikers/people in general! Whenever I would go to check it out, he was exactly right about the mess. He usually appeared very quickly and didn't stay long in my dreams. He was direct and to the point. Beau, another betta, always assisted me by joining me in my nighttime dreams and astral travels. He had a very psychic connection to the glaciers located in the arctic circle, and he often encouraged me to send supportive healing to them since global warming was causing them to vanish. We would send different types of energy to the ice caps that were melting. Even if some of them still melted, we would visualize the water slowly making its way down to areas where humans were more populous and would program the water with a sense of urgency. The goal was for the water to affect any humans it came into contact with and make them feel urgently connected to protecting ice caps and stopping global warming.

I no longer become sad when one of my fish passes into the next life because they are always with me. Souls never truly die; they just change form and move on to the next experience they choose. In the case of incarnated merpeople, they just go back to the astral mermaid realm. This means that I can visit them and dream with them often. We can still work on projects together psychically and assist each other's spiritual journeys. When merpeople incarnate in fish bodies, I think that it helps people in human bodies make connections to the mermaid realm. Even after the merperson leaves the Earth plane, there is a permanent connection that can never be lost or severed.

The relationships I have with my merfish are some of the most sacred I have experienced in this life, but they are not rare or unique. Other incarnated mermaids on Earth have reported experiences similar to mine. Mermaids and mermen who incarnate on this planet usually live far away from each other, but even without having contact with each other while growing up, they all share the same behaviors and affinity for creating kinship with watery life.

CHAPTER 5

Forming Friendships with Ordinary Fish

The friendships I just described with my fish and with astral merpeople are possible for everyone, but they are especially possible for people who are focusing on making the water element within themselves stronger.

To a merperson, there are two types of fish (or aquatic creatures). One is the kind that I introduced you to in the previous chapter: a merperson who has taken the form of a fish for a short amount of time in our world. The second kind are ordinary fish. Ordinary fish do not have the auras of merpeople and are not incarnated merpeople. You do not need an incarnated merperson in a fish body to develop friendships with fish. Even the most common fish will happily be your companions if you create a space filled with positive energy and a nice home for them.

My ordinary fish are just as special as my merfish because they still bring the watery element into my living space, and they are spiritual beings all on their own. I spend large amounts of time standing over their tanks talking to them and calling them by name. I play my ukulele softly for them, and the sound vibrations create ripples in the water that they can feel.

Some of my fish have favorite songs. I named one of my Oranda fish Calypso because she became extremely excited and overfriendly when I plucked out John Denver's "Calypso" over her tank. The more time I spend with fish (common and magical), the more I realize that they each have personalities, desires, dreams, and needs just like we do.

Because fish are unable to speak with voices or make human facial expressions, it is easy to assume that they do not have feelings or the capacity to love as we do, when nothing could be further from the truth. When my golden retriever died and I felt sad, I went into my room and leaned my head against my Oranda tank (that also contained Black Moors), and all six of my fish came and pressed their lips to the other side of the glass.

Thinking that they wanted food, I dumped some in their tank. They all watched it float around for a minute, but not one of them left their post at the other side of the tank until I backed away from the glass and they knew that I was okay.

Orandas are a type of goldfish, and goldfish have excellent memories. They can remember patterns, people, and the way that you make them feel, and they are only one species of fish. Imagine the great capacity in the aquatic kingdom for various characteristics and capabilities. I do not feel that my fish owe me any sort of service or work. They deserve to live happy lives in great tanks with plenty of stimulation and fun without my getting anything from them. Still, there are many benefits and possibilities when making friends with fish.

I like to know what the birth dates of my fish are because their astrological sun signs tend to be a clear indication of why they came to be in my life. A fish with a sun sign in Cancer usually needs a lot of quality time with me and a strong community of other fish around them (provided that it is a species that can be housed with others). A fish's astrological sign can also be an indicator of its personality and can tell you how to nurture its mental and emotional needs on a deeper level. Sometimes it is not possible to know exactly what your fish's birth chart looks like, but a lot of observation on your part can usually guide you to a really good guess.

All merpeople love fish and any other creatures that dwell in water. If you are attracted to sea stars, jellyfish, or even sea slugs more than fish, that is okay. All of these beings can form friendships and relationships with you. Remember that aquatic souls (whether they are mer or not) are connected to the mer-realm on some level, and they receive love in the form of energy. Sending love to your sea slug is investing in the mermaid realm just as much as talking to an astral merperson and telling them you love them.

CHAPTER 6

How to Build a Mer-realm

In this chapter, I would like to discuss the magical and practical friendships that are possible when you are building your own mermaid kingdom. While my first merman came to me of his own accord without my planning our meeting or expecting it, these sorts of interactions with mermen in fish bodies are not limited to people who do not expect it. It is possible for someone to ask the mermaid realm for an ally from the mer-realm to come to them in the form of a fish or aquatic creature; however, the person asking must have a good reason for doing so.

For example, if you say, "I want a mermaid to incarnate in a fish body so that I can feel cool," it is unlikely that the mer-realm is going to satisfy that request. It takes a lot of energy for a merperson to maintain physical form, and the life of a betta fish is simple and plain. It would be unfair to ask a magical creature to incarnate just for your own enjoyment. If you were to say, "I want to fill the Earth with love and joy and share this vibration with the world by mastering the water element," you are likely to get some response from the mermaid realm. But even if you do not have a merperson inside a fish body living with you, you can still build a mermaid kingdom with regular fish and ground the physical element of the mermaid realm into your day-to-day life.

My room and home are filled with fish tanks and water-based life. At the end of a long day, I feel as if I am stepping back into the mermaid realm when I enter my bedroom. It instantly restores anything that the world has drained out of me. Mermaids and mermen exist in fish bodies in my room, but I also have a wide variety of fish that are not incarnated merpeople, and they too assist me with psychic work.

Mermen tend to come to me in the form of koi fish and betta fish more than any other type of fish. The merpeople have told me that the reasons for this are that these fish types are easily accessible and live in freshwater. I have had merpeople come to me in the form of marine life, but most appear as freshwater fish.

Merpeople choose freshwater because this is the type of water that exists in human bodies, and it helps the merpeople to focus on the water that is more native to human beings. It is what humans drink, and it is easier to do work from within a freshwater matrix when healing people or focusing on upgrading the consciousness of world leaders.

As I mentioned in an earlier chapter, there is a twofold process to developing a mermaid kingdom. One is physical, and one is spiritual, with the spiritual being more important by far. However, I do not want to disregard the merits of creating your own shoal of fish to return to when you go home.

Building Your Physical Mermaid Kingdom

You can start small with your physical mermaid kingdom. One betta fish or a small community tank of goldfish is enough to bring the water element to your living space. You can enjoy the companionship and natural gifts that every fish has to offer, or you can invite a merperson to join you through a fish in your community. Having a merperson inhabit a fish's body does not harm the fish. It simply enhances their consciousness.

Remember, the closer we are in vibration to the mermaid realm, the more we draw it into our experience. Though most of the work is spiritual, it helps me to have an aesthetically pleasing environment that acts as a conduit for the energy (and everyone knows mermaids love pretty things). My room and home are filled with colors that bring a sense of magic to my awareness. My room is painted with ocean blues, purples, and hints of pink (because pink carries the vibration of love).

I have massive collections of shells, crystals, and fish fossils on display. I like to feel connected to all stages of evolution regarding oceanic life, so fossils are important for me to have nearby. I moved most of my books into a separate room and created a library with its own space because sometimes having too many books in a room can overshadow the consciousness of the subtle water element.

I love to listen to the sound that all of my aquarium fil-
ters make while I go to sleep at night. Hearing the sound of
the mermaid element running all around me helps me sleep
even better. Some people choose to buy waterbeds, wave pro-
jectors, the music of ocean waves, and mermaid artwork to
put in their homes to keep them in the spirit of the water
element.

If you travel often or have an extremely busy life and cannot be a keeper of fish, that is okay. All of this is entirely up to
you. This is your mermaid kingdom, and only you can decide
exactly what nurtures your spiritual development and understanding of the water element.

Make sure that you feel at peace in the space where you
do the majority of your meditations, and if you do have fish
that you bring with you during meditation, make sure that it
is a comfortable place for them, too.

It is also possible for you to create a space out in nature
if you do not have your own room or you just do not like
meditating indoors. Choosing a stream, pool, or section of
a river to meditate by is part of your spiritual journey and
your choice should be made wisely. Choose a space that feels
beautiful and relaxing to you where you can be undisturbed
during meditations. If you live far enough away from hikers
and other people, you can leave small crystals or shells in your
usual spot and allow them to anchor in mermaid energy when
you are gone.

Wherever your mermaid kingdom is located on Earth,
what is important is that it is your own space. Merpeople
will automatically connect to your consciousness no

matter where you are during your meditations. Your level of safety, relaxation, and focus are key to how clearly communication occurs.

Building Your Spiritual Mermaid Kingdom

Building your own spiritual mermaid kingdom requires inner work. Developing empathy, unconditional love, and a feeling of always being complete in yourself can take time. Humans are often raised to be codependent and self-serving, but psychic abilities such as telepathy and clairvoyance can be developed after the empathetic groundwork is laid.

I personally advise people to begin doing the exercises in Franz Bardon's *Initiation into Hermetics.* The exercises in his book can help individuals refine their focusing abilities so that they can be conscious recipients of divine messages. Another author, William Mistele, is a friend of mine who writes wonderful books about elementals. He offers essays, short stories, novels, and videos that focus on the basics for developing mermaid empathy. He also offers free instruction on how to develop the skill of active listening (a skill that merpeople perform wonderfully).

Connecting with a merperson can become an important part of your spiritual experience Even if you are nowhere near fish or water right now, you can invite a merperson to be with you in spirit form. In the exercise below, we are going to invite an astral merperson to be your companion in the form of an aquatic creature.

🐟 Meditation to Invite a Merperson in Spirit Form

Sit or lie down in a comfortable area in any position that feels good to you. I think it is fun to do this meditation while sitting in the bathtub or in a creek, but wherever you want to be is perfect. You may ask your spirit guides to be with you for protection and support.

Start by taking several deep breaths. Feel yourself relaxing as any tension leaves your muscles. Relax your jaw and let your eyes soften. Close your eyes gently to rest them. You do not need your physical eyes right now. You will be using your spiritual eye and your own intuition to "see" what you desire.

Focus on your energy for a moment or the few feet of space surrounding your physical body. This space contains your aura or personal energy field. Human auras can come in many shapes, colors, sizes, and textures. Imagine your aura becoming a cool layer of liquid water around your body.

Take your time to feel this, and visualize it around you. The water can be clear or a green-blue, salt water or fresh. Feel this water become part of you, extending outward and expanding slowly until it seems as if it is a giant "bubble" of water around you. The water may fluctuate or have a gentle current.

Focus on your emotions. Let go of any anger, frustration, or deadlines you have been focused on today. We are in a space of timelessness and presence. Be here now, and allow yourself to be caressed by the water around you.

Now, begin to imagine what your companion is like. On a physical level, do they look like a fish, a sea star, an octopus, or an aquatic creature you have dreamed up? Imagine every detail. The guide you are attracting may show up suddenly in your mind's eye or you may want to build your companion slowly, piece by piece.

Mentally, what does this being feel like? Are they able to tap into your thoughts and share mental images telepathically with you? Are they emotionally connected to you as well, and do you feel connected to them? What does their aura feel like? Most astral water companions are very loving and devoted to becoming one with the person who invites them in or creates them. Are they able to look inside your heart and understand your deepest dreams and talk to you about them?

After you have a clear feeling and image of what your companion is like, imagine pulling them into the water bubble surrounding your body (your aura). Usually, your new friend will just jump into the water you have created around yourself. It is their natural element, and they feel most at home there. This is where your friend will remain. They will be part of you and will always be accessible whenever you need them.

This is how you invite an astral merperson into your life. Even if you feel that you create them out of nothing, their consciousness already exists in the mermaid realm. You just give them form and allow them to come to you.

Anything is possible with your new merfriend. You can have relationships like the ones I have had with my magical fish, you can work on psychic projects, and you can ask them for support when you need it. Astral companions are practical because they do not require special care or attention in the way merpeople inside physical fish bodies do. The exchange of emotion and thought is their currency, and since they are connected to you, they will always be there whenever you need to touch base with the mermaid realm.

Neptune (a later incarnation of Dante) is now my astral companion, and I see him dart in and out of my aura sometimes during the day. Your new contact from the mer-realm may eventually start to feel like a soul mate to you as they become a perfect mirror for your state of being. They are a permanent part of your spiritual mermaid kingdom.

My regular fish provide comfort and feel emotions in addition to holding a space for the physical aspect of water. My merfish are like this as well but with far more awareness. My merfish are able to enter my dreams, send healing energy to people that I meditate on, and come to me in visions when I am away from them.

One night, while I was away from home and wide awake in the mountains, I saw one of my betta fish appear ethereally in front of me. He said, "I have to go now, but I'll be back." When I got home, he had passed away from old age.

Merpeople in fish bodies are able to appear at will in front of humans (in a ghostly, etheric form), and they usually do this by entering our dreams when we are asleep so as not to scare us. In this way, merpeople are able to send messages, share energy, and talk to our spiritual body while we are asleep, so dream communication (lucid dreaming) is a useful skill for humans wishing to connect to the mer-realm.

Merpeople in fish bodies are able to imprint water, as you learned how to do in chapter 2. They appreciate it when you imprint their water when you clean it or do weekly water changes. If the currency of the average human is paper money or coins, then the currency of the mer-realm is energy exchange. When you give a feeling or a positive thought to a merperson, they return it tenfold.

The merpeople are here to assist me in helping others to integrate the water element into their personalities. My mermen have shown me that part of my mission on planet Earth is to support and heal people by positively affecting their physical and spiritual water.

Humans have five elements available to them: fire, water, earth, air, and akasha (spirit). Water represents empathy, nurturing energy, and love, and sometimes it can be particularly weak in people who power through life with an indomitable will. Almost everyone has a weak element. Mine is fire. It is our spiritual mission to bring all of the elements into balance within ourselves.

In contrast to humans with five elements in their souls, many spirits of nature (called elementals) have souls composed of just one element. Thus you would contact a merperson to learn about water, a sylph to learn about air, a salamander to learn about fire, a gnome to learn about earth, and so on.

One of my favorite things to do with my magical fish is to work on the water in the bodies of government leaders. It's also one of the most common exercises I do. Merpeople are against any sort of violence or force, and I share their feelings. People in positions of power are under immense stress, and that can affect the decisions that they make. We always ask permission from the person's astral body first, and usually, we receive permission to send a watery download in the direction of our recipient.

I usually sit next to my fish in their aquarium during this gentle meditation. First, we imbue spiritual water with whatever feeling we are wishing to send to someone, and then we visualize it becoming part of them. That is really all there is to it, but the exercise can yield powerful results over time. It can help people develop empathy and consider the impacts their decisions have on everyone around them. This exercise can be used on anyone, anywhere, at any time.

Another project that the merpeople and I like to work on is cleaning up our environment and getting trash out of our water systems. Sometimes this requires meditating on people who decide that dumping chemical waste into the water system is a good idea; other times it requires us to send healing energy to the water itself. The merman or mermaid that assists me amplifies the energy that I send out and provides companionship and support during the process.

During meditations that I do for global water cleanliness

and ocean cleanup, all of my merpeople join in on the meditation to make it extra powerful. They will usually be hovering as close to me as they can get with a very focused look on their fish faces.

Magical fish have psychic abilities, as well as many more abilities that are yet to be discovered. Spending quality time with all of your fish is important to building relationships with them and with the mer-realm. Fish and all aquatic life are part of the mermaid realm. Inviting them in, whether or not they are incarnations of the astral world, will enhance your mermaid experience and help you constantly immerse in the merworld.

CHAPTER 7

The Astral Mer-realm

The mermaid realm, located on the astral plane, has a pure, watery vibration that embodies nurturing love. Some people believe that only highly trained individuals can enter the mermaid realm. Others believe that anyone who wants to connect with mermaids can gain access.

Mermaids want humans to be part of their realm and love to invite them into this sacred space. However, the realm is guarded by astral protectors (gorgon medusas, described in chapter 9, about astral allies). The purpose of these guardians is to make sure that anyone who goes into the mermaid realm has good intentions. These protectors also ensure it is healthy for humans to go into the mermaid realm and look out for their well-being while they are there.

For some, the mermaid realm is so beautiful and enchanting that they want to abandon their human lives to become part of it. This is something that the mermaid realm tries to prevent. Mer-realm guardians help these individuals come back to their physical bodies and feel grounded again. The purpose of being human is to bring benefits to the human world and to assist this planet in its evolution. Staying in the mermaid realm when we have a mission in our own world is not allowed.

Most people are allowed within the first area of the mermaid realm. It is a watery space with beautiful, shimmering colors where merpeople and fish can swim up to you for a conversation. Deeper within the realm are other areas that hold mysteries and magic.

The thing to remember when entering magical realms is that your core vibration is what allows you to access a certain space. If you are trying to enter a highly evolved space while you are thinking dense, hateful thoughts, you will not even be able to perceive the higher dimensions while you are in them. Who you choose to be is the most important decision you can make. Sometimes humans are denied access to the mermaid realm when appearing to be too needy or seeking an escapist's route from reality. Making sure that your emotional and mental bodies are in balance before deciding to go on an astral road trip is always a great idea. Chakra balancing exercises, healing old hurts, resolving inner conflict, and knowing your strengths and weaknesses will help you be the best version of yourself that you can be.

Upon entering the mermaid realm, there are many options available to the astral traveler. Merpeople may come to you and lead you to certain areas, or you may be given permission to explore specific parts of their realm.

One of my favorite areas is something I affectionately call the playroom, literally a place where you can swim with the mermaids and play with them. It is a space that embodies the celebratory and jubilant spirit of the mermaid realm, and sometimes you can even hear the mermaids sing their songs. Sometimes humans come here when they dream at night and then forget about it after they wake up.

One of my first dreams in the playroom launched me into the "shallower" regions of the water. Light was filtering through the water's surface, and I was sitting on a glittering sand bed about twenty feet below. I started to rest my eyes and feel the crystalline grains beneath me twinkling some cute musical notes. That is when I sensed something pass over my head. I opened my eyes to see a mermaid with an extremely long tail. She swam down to me and handed me something that sparkled in the light.

"Put it on," she said, while smiling at me.

I took a closer look at what she had handed me and realized it was a mermaid tail. It was a soft pink that blended into iridescent whites and golds. Each scale was accented with a pearl so pure that it changed color every time it moved. The pearls were like faceted diamonds with the ability to be many colors at once.

I quickly slipped on the mermaid tail and noticed how light it felt. I did not feel as if I had legs anymore. The mermaid tail became part of me and fit me perfectly. It felt as silky as the water around me, and I glided with a gentle current for a few seconds.

"Follow me," said the mermaid.

I began to try to kick my "legs" to catch up to her. She turned around and laughed with a sound that closely resembled music. Hovering above my head, she pointed to her abdomen and showed me how to flex with that area of my body and undulate my entire tail to move forward.

Mermaid swimming lessons are priceless. After this I was able to swim easily behind her as we explored underwater caves and swam through kelp forests. I saw some funny things while I was swimming around in this space, too, such as other humans learning how to swim with tails and a school of fish having a race through a kelp forest.

The playroom differs from the initial reception area in that it is a place for recreation rather than discussion. You might hear a passing giggle, a whale's call, or the sound of bubbles underwater, but serious conversations concerning the fate of humanity and planet Earth are held in other places. If you are interested in visiting a space that facilitates light-hearted connection with merfolk, please enjoy the following meditation.

🐟 Meditation to Enter the Mer-realm

I would like to invite you into the mer-realm. Here you will find love, joy, and kindness. This is an invitation from the merpeople to be more like them and to join them in celebrating the beauty of the water element on Earth.

I would advise that you do a chakra balancing meditation before joining me on this journey. There are many chakra meditations on YouTube and in books if you wish to engage in a momentary detoxification process. The chakra balancing will ensure that you are spiritually, emotionally, and physically balanced so that this voyage feels good to you. When you feel good, you attract even more experiences that feel good. Put simply, chakra balancing is aligning yourself with what is positive and creative and stepping free of things that hold you back and weigh you down.

You should also make sure you are hydrated. It helps if the water you drink is imbued with the energy of love.

Now that you are clear and ready to go on an adventure, make sure that you are in a peaceful place where you will not be disturbed. You may lie down and relax if you wish as long as you feel that you will not fall asleep. You do not need any extra items for this journey, but if you want to cover yourself with a blanket or hold your favorite crystal while you travel, that is okay. Start by taking several deep breaths to relax. Now visualize cool, liquid water in your mind and imagine it running up and down your body. Take your time and notice every emotion, image, and sensation that arises. Allow the water to become part of you while maintaining your awareness of it in your body. You may feel a little chilled. This is normal. The astral realm is cold compared to the temperature of the human body.

When you feel ready, imagine your astral body. Your astral body is an exact image of your physical body, but it is less dense and expresses pure feeling. Now feel yourself slowly float out of your body through your crown chakra at the top of your head. You may feel as if you are floating or get a little bit dizzy. Take a moment to steady yourself and stabilize.

When you are ready, continue exiting your physical body until you can look down and see your physical body resting below. If you are having a hard time experiencing this, try visualizing another "you" in front of you that is going through these steps.

Once outside your body, float up farther and exit through the roof of your home. There is a mermaid and a merman on either side of your body ready to accompany you to their world. They each may take on whatever form is most appealing to you. They both gently clasp your forearms with their hands and begin to pull you upward into a space of soft light.

If you are looking down, you may see that the world below is starting to look a little bit hazy. This is good. It means that you are exiting the human world and shifting to a different dimension. Allow yourself to be carried forward into a space with soft white and aquamarine light. You may feel as if your feet are brushing against fluffy clouds or that your body is filled with great amounts of energy. This is all normal.

Every sensation you experience is real and is the mermaid realm attempting to establish contact with you. After a few moments of traveling toward this light, you will arrive at an exotic gateway made of abalone and pearls (and any other gemstone you find attractive). At the gate stand some powerful guardians. They nod at the mermaid and merman on either side of you and move aside. The gate does not need to be opened. Since you are in astral form, you have the ability to pass right through it into the mermaid world beyond. The space beyond the gate looks heavenly, and maybe you can even see colors and hues that are brighter than the ones we see on Earth. Past some of the haze and initial colors, you may see some alluring blue-green pools of water with exotic fish swimming around in them. There are walkways for your benefit, though it feels as if you are floating. Beautiful sculptures of mermaids, gemstones, and colorful energy veils surround each pool of water.

Pause for a moment. Make a mental note of everything you see, smell, taste, hear, and feel. One of the purposes of this meditation is for you to explore. Take your time to look around and notice what the mermaid realm feels like. Can you sense your own aura here? Would you like to sit down by one of the magical pools and take a peek at all of the unique-looking water creatures in them? You are allowed to step in if you like.

You might see some other humans on astral journeys here. Feel free to talk to them or to speak with your own merguides that helped you get here. Certain people choose to seek advice regarding general matters of love and oneness while here.

It is common to be overcome with powerful waves of

emotion and pleasant feelings when you first get to the mermaid realm. It is like entering heaven, and some of the burdens of your human life may fall away and leave you feeling lighter and freer than you have in a while. The mermaid realm is very addicting because it makes a person feel fully alive.

When you are ready, you will travel to the next level of the mermaid realm. This is called the playroom, and it is an enticing, watery space where humans and other galactic species come to interact with the mermaid realm. Feel yourself moving forward, past the courtyard of the mermaids. On the horizon, there is a body of water that looks like a silvery-blue streak of shimmering light. This is where you are going.

Between you and this oceanic oasis is a white sand beach. It is so white that it is almost glassy where the perfect blue and white hues of the mermaid realm are mirrored back to you. Sometimes an astral jellyfish will float by and cast its fuchsia hue onto the glassy beach, making the panorama explode with even more color. Enjoy the scenery and the way it makes you feel. Everything here feels fully alive.

Every grain of sand between your toes has a spiritual journey and a sparkling story to tell. Some of the grains of sand may stick to your feet and look like glittering diamonds as you come to the edge of the water. This water is unlike any water you have ever seen. It is practically bioluminescent and glowing with a life of its own.

Go ahead and step into the water. Your mermaid and merman guide will wait on the glassy beach for you and will escort you once more when you are finished here. The ground beneath your feet slopes gently downward and gets deeper the farther you go out. You do not need to be afraid of drowning here. No one can drown in the astral realm. You may find that you do not even need to breathe underwater. Every astral molecule here is feeding your body with its vitality, and because of this, there is no need for oxygen. However, you may still breathe if you wish to pull the essence of this space into your lungs.

Walk down the gentle slope of sand into the water. When you are at chest level with the water, you may begin to swim if you like. Dive down into the water, and go deeper into the realm. It is bigger than the sky and seems to go on forever. Do not worry about getting lost. Your mermaid and merman guides will assist you if you ask. This is where your most adventurous self may take over. You can explore giant kelp forests, sculpt a lute out of ancient coral, befriend colorful fish, play with other humans, or talk to mermaids you encounter. This is called the playroom for a reason, and you are allowed to do whatever you like.

We are in the astral realm, so you may imagine that

you have a mermaid tail. Your tail can look any way you want it to—any color, any shape, any size. You simply need to look down to see it.

Anything you experience in the mermaid realm is a reflection of your current understanding of the water element. The more fun, playful, and loving it is the more you are in tune with the heart of the mermaid kingdom.

Take your time to explore this new world, but when you are ready to leave this place, all you need to do is think or say, "I am ready to leave," and your mermaid and merman guides will instantly be there to assist you in leaving the water.

When you are ready to leave the mer-realm, all you have to do is say so, and you can begin to reenter your physical body. Wiggle your fingers and toes, and sit up slowly.

I suggest eating a snack and drinking some water upon your return. Feel your bare feet on the earth to feel grounded and connected to the human world again. It is important to reconnect before driving or doing strenuous physical activity. You can access the mermaid playroom at any time. If you become adept at lucid dreaming, you can make use of the many hours you spend sleeping to be productive and integrate the mermaid realm into your consciousness.

CHAPTER 8

My Experiences
with Astral Mermaids

I have briefly mentioned that astral mermaids began appearing to me in the bathtub and in my dreams when I was a young girl. Those interactions only brush the surface of what I have since experienced with my astral mermaid family.

When I first met astral mermaids, I did not know any of their names. When I was with them, I always forgot to ask because I was so excited to be with them. After I met another author friend who has written several books about mermaids, I discovered that one of the mermaids who visits me the most often is named Isaphil and that she is a lunar mermaid spirit (a moon spirit). She is described briefly in Franz Bardon's book *The Practice of Magical Evocation*.

When I was a preteen, I used to listen to Isaphil talk about who she was and how she experienced reality. She would always hum or sing the line, "I am the sea . . . I am the sky . . . I am the stars that shine," in a lovely soprano voice. She said that she would teach me the art of feminine tranquility by giving me poetry and prose to communicate ideas.

Here is one of her compositions, in which she speaks with the voice of moonlight shining in water.

> *Does an iceberg need to breathe? Does the moon*
> *have a heartbeat? The moon does not lose her*
> *grace when the sun no longer shines on her*
> *face;*
> *She does not wait for the next day or have a*
> *thought to anticipate.*
> *Is there a plan in the ocean's spray or desire in*
> *volcanic lakes?*
> *Be still. I am suspended between the inhale and*
> *the exhale; between the ebb and the flow.*
> *This is a place where you can be so clear that pain*
> *and even thoughts disappear.*
> *When you place your hand upon my face, you will*
> *feel the oceans of the Earth as one wave. This*
> *is a gift from the sea and the foundation of all*
> *peacemaking.*
> *The biggest problem faced by man is to see dreams*
> *as whimsical things rather than states of being.*
> *There are dreams inside me so sweet that they*
> *end all separation and heal every being.*
> *Release identity and live so free that fear and*
> *thought have no way to distract from all that*

is and all you can be. Now is the key. In your
dreams, become the answer you ask for.

Eclipsed in your mind is a great enigma: Your
dreams are the lifeboats for your Earthly
expeditions. Stillness is the seaport for your
thoughts craving repose. My love will ferry you
across the expanse.

When you are so endless and serene that all that
exists is in your being, then your very existence
will create peace and be like the waves and
tides that reflect lunar light.

In every moment, we arrive. Innocence is being in
this one moment knowing it is the first, the
last, and the eternal without forgetting and
losing the miracle you are.

There is a portal named Serenity. As soon as you
enter it, you are at home. There is only here.
Stillness is the answer to your mystery.

I have asked Isaphil what people can do to connect with her energy or with the energy of other merpeople in her realm. I asked her for a simple solution to feel connected to mermaids.

She replied, "Quiet your mind, and feel the love in your heart that permeates the universe. Create a space in your heart where you can feel love for everything that exists. When you love as we do, you are one of our own."

I then asked her, "Do you have any advice for someone who is finding it hard to love so unconditionally?"

Isaphil told me, "We are all one drop of the same wave. When you no longer see yourself as separate from others and understand that oneness is just a state of being, you will love as we do."

I thanked her for sharing her heart with me. Isaphil provided wonderful guidance then and has continued to do so since.

CHAPTER 9

Astral Allies in the Mer-realm

Astral allies are regarded as mythological beings in our world. They are very powerful and work closely with the mermaid realm. Though they are independent of the human race, they are willing to lend assistance to those with the right motivation. If you wish to gain their support, you need to be able to prove that you are of a certain level of maturity and capability. You will also need to make a good case as to why you should receive their help. Spirits will respect you more if you come to them with a request that benefits both of you.

Astral allies are not entirely loving like mermaids are. They are neither mean nor loving. They are what they are, and sometimes that can be scary. Humans like to put things into categories and boxes, and that simply does not work for spirits that live in the astral realm. They are under no obligation to conform to our sense of morality or to prove themselves to us. However, with a good cause and an ability to interact flexibly with beings who are very different from us, communication and even friendship is possible with these magical creatures.

Here, I would like to introduce some astral allies I have encountered in my mermaid experience, share their stories, and discuss my interactions with them. This is not an all-inclusive guide—there are many allies and astral entities beyond the ones that I will discuss. I have selected those that I have interacted with the most and will share how I gained their respect and companionship.

When dealing with astral allies or entities in general, there are a few important things to consider. Number one is making sure that you know how to protect your own energy with visualization, willpower, and good technique for entering and exiting spiritual spaces. Learning how to open energetic doorways and close them properly will help prevent any contact with unwelcome entities. Sometimes even ghosts that used to be humans can come through open energetic doorways and become pests to the inexperienced magician or spiritual seeker. Asking your spirit guides to assist you and help you be aware of your spiritual surroundings is always helpful. Everyone on planet Earth has at least one spirit guide, and I strongly advise you to ask for their assistance before every magical endeavor.

Second, it is wise to make sure that your intentions for communicating with magical beings are crystal clear and refined so that you do not pester spirits needlessly.

Finally, come with your credentials. By that I mean that it is not the best idea to go start a chat with a gorgon medusa if this is week one for your personal magical training. Spirits do not have egos like humans do, but they do not like to be bothered by people who have no idea what they are doing with their own energy. You need to have some level of skill before contacting astral entities (other than spirit guides) so that you can keep yourself safe and receive the assistance that you are requesting.

You cannot lie to spirits. They do not listen to your words as much as they read your energy. An instant scan of your energy will provide them with knowledge about how skilled you are, how experienced you are, and even what your life's purpose is.

Krakens

The first entity I would like to introduce you to is a kraken. Krakens have been written about for centuries and are usually depicted as the attackers of large ships. In real life, krakens actually do look like giant octopi, and the kraken legend is usually related to the giant squids that exist in real life in our oceans today. But kraken allies are separate entities that exist in the astral realm.

Like most astral entities, krakens are widely misunderstood. It is natural for humans to fear things that we know little about. Unlike what happens in the stories about them, krakens do not usually sink ships or chase after people who bear "the black spot,"* but they can exist in astral (spirit) form on our ocean floor and can exert real influence on our physical ocean.

---

*In old pirate tales, someone would be given a black spot, and shortly after, a sea monster would come and kill them or a person would simply drop dead. A few examples of the legend appear in *Treasure Island* by Robert Louis Stevenson, in which people had a black spot delivered to them by a messenger, and in the *Pirates of the Caribbean* movie, in which victims had the spot appear on their hand and Davy Jones's kraken would come for them.

I began dreaming with krakens several years ago when I first entered adulthood. In one of my dreams, I was swimming in the ocean when I felt this sucking sensation at my feet that felt like an extremely strong vacuum. It felt as though it was trying to pull me underwater, so I panicked. I kicked and flailed and tried to get away. The sucking sensation stopped for a moment, and I suddenly realized that I was in a dream (which made it a lucid dream).

Since I knew I was dreaming, I understood that I could not die, so I decided to stop fighting and see where the sucking sensation would take me. I stopped resisting and started being pulled underwater. It seemed as if I would never reach the bottom. I must have floated downward several thousand feet before I finally landed at the bottom of the ocean floor.

In real life, my body would have been crushed by the weight of the water, but things work differently in the spirit world, and we are able to access areas that are not necessarily possible for our human bodies. Even though I was far enough away from the surface for it to be pitch black, I was able to see due to the aura of the water molecules I was immersed in. Spirit water glows for me, and I never experience total darkness while underwater in the astral realm because of that quality.

After I landed at the bottom, I became aware of a giant mass in front of me. It looked like a muted purple mountain until it reached one of its arms toward me and pulled me closer. I realized that I was staring up at a giant octopus. I stood (well, floated) completely still for a few seconds while the kraken scanned my energy. I think it was deciding whether I would be able to understand it. Then it placed one of its tentacles on my third eye chakra between my eyebrows. What I experienced next is hard to describe. I did not necessarily hear a voice talking to me, but I felt vibrations go straight through my body that translated into words in my brain.

The kraken said, "You have been called here because it is time to reveal my purpose and why I came into being."

"In our world, researchers have compared the great octopi to extraterrestrials. Is that the nature of your origin?" I asked.

The kraken continued to tell me his story. "I remember when the stars came into existence and the Earth began to form. The Earth is even older than many of you suspect, and my consciousness bloomed when it began to take form. I existed in other realms before the Earth came to be, but I was part of a collective, and now I experience reality as a singular entity.

"I observed the occurrence of Earth's formation for millions of years and became fascinated by the idea of understanding how life unfolds. This was the first time I was close to 3rd density, you see. I leaned against the veil of higher dimensions and pressed my 'nose against the glass,' as you might say. . . . I could not look away from the great story unfolding before me. I was given the divine commission to keep records of every death at sea and every movement across the ocean floor. I came into being with the ability to clear the ocean floor of long-held debris and remember every detail and speck of anything that touches my domain. When I observed the birth and death of stars while Earth was still forming, I became acquainted with what your scientists call black holes. When an object gets too close to the event horizon of a black hole, it is sucked in, and not even light can escape.

"I began pondering these things in my heart as I recorded every shell and oceanic creature that fell to and decayed on my ocean floor. After I started my commission of keeping the records of happenings on the ocean floor, I also began to experiment with the idea of sending my records and memories to other points in time and transporting giant masses of debris from the ocean floor to other places.

"This is why some ships that have sunk in the oceans have never been found, even when they sank in shallow areas. My consciousness can create giant whirlpools in the ocean. Though your scientists cannot yet perceive it, I use my whirlpools to transport long-held matter into alternate dimensions and to beam information to other parts of the galaxy. Dolphins and other creatures that make their home in my oceans have ancestral origins on other planets. By creating energetic links and information pathways to other planets and parts of the universe, I invite more attention to life on Earth and ensure that no matter how many times the ocean is assaulted by weather conditions or the human race, some inhabitants will always survive.

"Sometimes I help certain species leave the ocean through my whirlpools and transport them to a safe place elsewhere in space-time. When danger has passed and other species have been nearly wiped out, I am sometimes able to use my whirlpools to suck the species I saved back into the ocean. This is why certain species that are thought to have been extinct can sometimes appear again with little to no explanation. This is my commission and why I came to be."

I found his story absolutely incredible and had to know more. "May I ask how you can aid humans as they awaken to their full potential?"

The kraken explained, "Those who have a purpose in preserving life on Earth and learning about the history of the sea may always find a mentor in me. Do not come blindly. You must be knowledgeable about the life patterns within the ocean and be free of attachment, lest you drown in sorrow with the memories of all who have passed in my realm. When you have mastered these things, you may call me a friend, and together we will preserve the story of every being that graces our domain. I can recall memories that are not yet retrievable by your current methods in science and help humans understand how life on Earth came into being."

I learned from my encounter that krakens seem to have a very specific mission when it comes to balancing oceanic ecosystems and preserving life that could easily be destroyed. Next, I would like to introduce you to an astral ally that has a more general mission.

Gorgon Medusas

Gorgon medusas are beings who act as guardians for the mermaid realm. Gorgon medusas appear to be similar to the way artists often depict them: with hair made of snakes (or eels) and exaggerated body curves. The protection they provide does not come from their snake hair. It comes from carefully directed energy and shielding techniques that they use to keep the mermaid realm and specific people from danger.

The gorgon medusas' mission is simple: protect incarnated mermaids and do not let unprepared visitors enter the mermaid realm. The mermaid realm is not something that anyone can destroy or take away. It is an immortal plane on the astral realm that holds a vibration that is immune to attack. However, the mermaid realm can cause problems for people who want to use it to escape or to gratify selfish needs. Gorgon medusas help to weed out the individuals who would try to bother mermaids in the realm. They can also be temporary guardians of an incarnated merperson on planet Earth, and I have experienced their protection.

I once had to go to court for a minor civil issue. Since my aura has water in it, I have attracted a great many more stalkers in my twenty-something years than most people do in an entire lifetime. Watery auras contain great magnetism, and they draw in people from all walks of life.

It is easy for imbalanced individuals to become obsessed with mermaids. Knowing this and being aware that the judge I would be talking to was known to give people a tough time, I asked the gorgon medusas to send one of their own to add some extra protection in advance.

The day that I went into court was unlike anything I had ever experienced. Men who normally would have harassed me dove out of my way in the parking lot. The secretary of the superior court offered me her assigned parking space while looking nervously at me for my approval. The judge who had a reputation for being rough on younger people (even in simple civil cases) was a perfect gentleman who kept asking me if there was anything else he could do to help me. A gorgon medusa was a little bit intense for the minor court appearance I made, but it gave me incredible insight into what these great beings are capable of.

Gorgon medusas tend to scare people senseless. Even if someone cannot see a gorgon medusa hovering next to a mer-person they are temporarily looking after, their presence is easily felt. Since they are invisible to most people, the humans we interact with assume that the nervous or scared feeling they are experiencing is coming from us when in fact it is the gorgon medusa.

Someone asked me why I do not permanently have a gorgon medusa in my energy field, and there are a couple of good answers for that. One is that my aura is not dense enough to keep a gorgon medusa near me for very long. I have a very ethereal version of the water element, and gorgon medusas tend to need something a little more grounded in the physical world to stick around. They are one of the few astral allies that need some level of density to accomplish their mission. Having a watery aura is what helps gorgon medusas make the link to our energy.

The second reason I do not have a medusa around to protect me all of the time is that having a gorgon medusa in one's energetic space for more than a couple of days can cause severe mood swings and emotional frustrations. Being around the intense energy field of a gorgon medusa does not affect the human body positively. Because of this, they should only be called on in extreme situations where one needs serious protection.

Selkies

Selkies are astral allies that can take on the form of seals. Selkies are wonderful counselors if one wishes to build a mermaid kingdom or create a mermaid family. Relationships and family are very important to selkies, and they make excellent instructors for people who are looking for a group or a club that will help them refine their magical skills. Though selkies are intelligent and highly observant, they function with somewhat of a hive mentality. They tend to work together in groups, and each selkie has a gift or piece of wisdom that they contribute.

Selkies are also playful and quirky. If you want to receive advice from one, it helps if you are in good humor and feel like socializing. They are also very adept at helping mermaids make their auras more attractive. The selkies' help means more people are drawn to mermaids and in turn come closer to the water element, a plus for these very social beings. Selkies are the extroverts of the astral allies.

Hydras

Hydras are a type of sea snake or eel. They appear with many heads and can be as intimidating as gorgon medusas. While gorgon medusas guard the mermaid realm and go on personal missions to protect incarnated mermaids, hydras stay focused on protecting sea life in our oceans. If there is a deep underwater cold coral reef and a ship many meters above is dumping harmful things into the water, a hydra may send feelings of panic or fear to the people on board to get them to move away from the corals or fish that need protection. Hydras are also responsible for many of the mishaps that have occurred when humans try to install underwater oil drilling rigs in the ocean. Hydras can teach students of magic how to use psychic energy to push people away from doing harmful things to the environment.

⁂

There are many astral allies you can connect with during your spiritual interactions with the watery realms. I have only listed a few here, but there are many more treasured friendships, alliances, and conversations to be had! The important thing is to respect your own limitations and to take the time to develop sensible relationships with any beings you contact. When you are ready, they will collaborate with you!

CHAPTER 10

Questions about Mermaids

While I've attempted to provide you with everything you need to know to begin connecting with mermaids, you may have some very specific questions that haven't yet been answered by this book. In the spirit of writing the owner's manual for mermaids that I wish I had as a child, I present some frequent questions and their answers here.

Questions about Mermaid Life

Do mermaids die?

Not if they are astral mermaids. These mermaids are immortal beings that reside on the astral plane. They do not experience death like we do. Their entire purpose is to be keepers of the water element. They are not bound to physical form, and they will continue to exist until the evolution of this universe is complete. However, mermaids in physical bodies will eventually experience the death of those physical bodies as we all do. Their immortal spirits return to the mermaid realm after the physical body is shed.

Do mermaids have children?

Unlike people in the physical world, mermaids do not have children on the astral plane. In that world, mermaids are already plentiful. Most mermaids have existed since Earth was formed. If for some reason the universe requires another keeper of water, the higher spirit realms are contacted and a new mermaid is sent forth. If a mermaid incarnates in a human body, then she *can* have human children.

Are merpeople physically intimate in the astral realm?

Merpeople do not need to make physical contact with each other to share love. They are not as dense or physical as we are and are able to share wonderful feelings through empathy and telepathy. In my dreams with merpeople, I have seen that while they are "swimming" around they sometimes lightly glide over each other and lightly brush tails or auras. This activity is not necessary, but it is one way that they interact with each other and within a community.

What do mermaids eat?

Astral mermaids do not need to eat food like we do. They are made of energy and are sustained by the vitality of their realm. Mermaids who incarnate need to eat since they are in physical bodies. Many that I have observed choose to become vegetarian or vegan because they have a lot of compassion for animals and do their best not to eat them.

Do astral mermaids need to sleep?

They do not require sleep like we do. Merpeople reside on the astral plane, and they do not have physical bodies in need of rest, though they do dream and travel the astral realm. If you see a mermaid embracing stillness and relaxing in a state of complete receptivity, she might look as if she is sleeping, but she is fully awake and aware. Going to the mermaid realm and experiencing life there as well as meditating with astral mermaids will provide you with valuable experience and insight into the watery element.

What do astral merpeople like to do the most? What are their favorite activities?

Each merperson has their own favorite activity, but all merpeople love to celebrate being alive and enjoy sharing love with everyone. They love to introduce people to their world and spend their "time" becoming masters of their particular skill with water (for example, one merman specializes in knowing the spiritual journey of every single pebble, molecule, creature, and algae bloom in his river).

Questions about Mermaid Characteristics

Do astral mermaids have tails or fins?

Mermaids are made of energy, and they can change their form when necessary. However, while they are in the mermaid realm, mermaids generally swim around with tails. The tails look a little bit different from what we normally imagine—they look less fishlike and are longer and more ethereal and wispy, more like long, beautiful energy trails that follow behind a mermaid's upper body. When we go to the mermaid realm, our preconceived ideas about what mermaids look like can affect what we see. Mermaids can appear in whatever form makes the most sense to us.

Do mermaids wear clothes or have an interest in fashion?

In the mermaid realm there is no shame surrounding nakedness. Nakedness is not equivalent to sexuality in their world, and they have no need for clothing. Mermaid women usually have extremely long hair that covers their breasts, but it is not for modesty purposes. Incarnated mermaids report that they do not like to wear clothing in our world because it messes with their energy. They can admire pretty clothing while they are here, but if given the choice, most of them would choose to be naked as often as possible.

Do merpeople have genders like humans do?

Yes and no. Mermaids and mermen are currently named based on whether their signature vibration is masculine or feminine from a human perspective. I have met merpeople who are a blend of the two energies and do not fit into just one gender or the other. Some merpeople may have gender identities that make sense to humans and others may not.

Do mermaids have beautiful voices?

Mermaids do have beautiful voices. Some mermaids live up to the ideal with beautiful singing voices, but all merpeople have the ability to create beautiful words and poems even if they do not sing or speak. The quality of their voices contains the power of their empathy and magnetism, and it makes them highly attractive.

Is mermaid empathy merely the ability to feel what others feel?

Think of it like this: A mermaid's aura extends outward like the magnetic field surrounding a magnet. Anything that passes through her aura she senses as if it were part of her own astral body. She can literally feel what you feel.

But mermaid empathy also means that they sense the deepest needs, desires, and dreams within you, and they equally sense the results—where and when in space and time that those things are fulfilled.

Mermaid empathy is not just receptive. It can send as well as receive. Some mermaids can also go into the future to see you as if they are looking at you in the present moment. Some can actually even create what it feels like to be your future self in the present moment so you can experience it. Then it is not just a matter of them asking, "Do you want to know your future?" It is them saying, "Here. Let me introduce you to yourself—the person you will one day be." But mermaids do not talk about this with words. They communicate it through the power of feeling.

This kind of empathy has the ability to connect directly to anyone on Earth, to modulate that individual's aura as if it is her own aura, to dissolve the negativity within the other, to heal, and to sense the other person so well that it is as if the other person is herself in another form.

Mermaid empathy has been hidden from us during the entire history of our civilization. It does feel what another feels. And it can also sense what has occurred in the past as well as the best outcome of what a person can become in the future. This is the nature of the vibration within water. There is no linear time. Everything—past, present, and future—is unfolding and fully alive in this moment of time.

What are some of the psychic abilities of mermaids?

Some of their psychic abilities are telepathy, extreme empathy, immortality, weather control, clairvoyance, seeing the future and the past, seeing auras, imbuing water with feelings and intentions, healing with water energy, speaking with spirits and the departed, and other abilities related to the magic of water.

Questions about Contacting Mermaids

Can you see mermaids in our oceans if you look hard enough?

Mermaids are spirits that are more ethereal than we are. Their bodies are less dense, which means that it is more challenging to see them than it is to see humans. It is possible to see mermaids near water or in our oceans with some clairvoyant ability or the right techniques. Spiritual sight can be developed and practiced just like any other skill. Feeling a mermaid presence is just as powerful and valid as seeing them with your eyes.

Do I need a special spell or potion to meet a mermaid?

No. Fortunately, meeting a mermaid is much easier than trying to find some magical potion. Doing the exercises in this book, connecting with the water element, and believing in mermaids makes it more likely that you will begin to dream with them and interact.

What is the best way to contact an astral merperson?

I think that the best way to make initial contact is by making the vibration of water part of yourself and also by learning how to lucid dream. There are many amazing books that can teach you how to become an adept lucid dreamer. Since souls travel to the astral realm while the body sleeps, it is easy to find the way to the mermaid realm and have fun experiences there.

Do mermaids have a written language?

They do not have a purpose for written language in their world since all thoughts and emotions are communicated automatically. Records do not need to be written down because merpeople have existed as long as water has, and they have perfect memories. However, when channeling mermaids, it is possible to translate their vibrations and energies into symbols and writing. In this sense, we can create written mermaid language on Earth. I have seen some examples of this on the internet, and the writing is extremely beautiful and elegant.

Are mermaids ever dangerous? Is contacting mermaids or traveling to their realm ever dangerous?

In and of themselves, mermaids are not dangerous beings. Problems can arise when humans fall in love with mermaids or their realm and do not want to leave. When a human abandons their body for too long, the body dies. This is why there are some restrictions on how much time certain people can spend in the mermaid realm.

In this book, I have been very clear that an individual should be motivated by a pure love and healthy respect for the wonder and beauty of nature. If an individual makes a serious effort to identify with the qualities of water—flowing; being receptive free of ego and selfishness; giving; seeking to heal, unite, and nurture—then an encounter with a mermaid is not so shocking or overpowering. The mer-realm is part of our own nature. It embodies one aspect of what we are to become.

All the same, there have been cases where direct contact with the astral plane can itself be a dangerous activity for those who are unprepared. Several individuals have found themselves shivering uncontrollably for hours or days after a strong contact with astral mermaids. In one example, a girl stopped her shivering by simply jumping into the ocean. The immersion in physical water reconnected her soul to her body. In another example, a male stopped shivering when someone gently massaged his physical body.

Also, through exposure to mermaids, an individual may lose his or her sense of weight and momentum. This is because when immersed in water, you feel weightless, so the sense of movement in space is suspended. You definitely do not want to drive a car or hike on steep trails until this sensation disperses.

Since there are no survival issues in the mermaid realm, exposure to the realm may also cause an individual to lose his survival instinct temporarily. He is no longer aware of danger. The loving aspect of water is good. But you have to find your own way of integrating it into your personality and life situation.

Questions about the Mer-realm

How big is the astral mermaid realm?

The mermaid realm cannot be measured in physical size like planets or cities, and it can expand or shrink to whatever size you imagine it to be. There are many areas within the mermaid realm, meaning that there are different vibrational spaces that are focused on different things. There are areas for healing, for studying the feminine mysteries, for interacting with lunar mansions, and so on.

The mermaid realm is centered around the idea of vibration rather than measurable dimensions. Just thinking about "empathy" will take you to an area different from thinking about the magnetism involved in intimate relationships.

Do astral mermaids ride seahorses or have pet fish in their realm?

Mermaids are able to appear wherever they want to within their realm just by thinking about the place they wish to go to. They do not need to ride seahorses or use transportation. Seahorse spirits do dwell within the mermaid realm, and they assist in maintaining the vibration of the realm. Mermaids in the astral realm do not think of fish as pets. They think of them as astral cocreators who can collaborate on psychic endeavors and preserve the water energy in the universe.

Do astral mermaids have a type of hierarchy?

Mermaids do not have power struggles or "higher or lower" mentalities. However, certain merpeople are more adept at certain skills than others. A mermaid may go to a certain merman if she wants to learn how to be more task oriented with a certain project. A merman may seek out a certain mermaid to learn the mysteries of stillness from her. Mermaid queens and kings are regarded as beings who have become total masters of their craft. Still, they are not seen as more valuable or superior than others in their world.

Are there different races of mermaids?

A mermaid is a mermaid no matter what. Mermaids do not have a need to categorize themselves like we do when we classify things. If you observe mermaids long enough, you might start to create the idea of "races" in your head if you divide them up by skill sets or by appearances, but in truth merpeople are all one race united by their watery composition. I have observed mermaids of all skin, eye, and hair colors. They all have their own unique features. One mermaid I have observed even had lavender eyes!

There are many other kinds of beings or creatures that are empathic and highly sensitive to water in nature. Some of these, for example, embody the spirits of various fish. In that fish can be territorial and aggressive, these beings have personality traits more associated with other animals or human beings than with the race of mermaids.

What is astral immortality?

Franz Bardon often used the phrase *astral immortality*. To him, it means an individual's astral body does not deteriorate but sustains its life independent from its environment. Typically, when an individual dies, his astral body slowly deteriorates. We see the same deterioration with living people as they age. They suffer trauma. They are forced to live under severe restrictions. They may be imprisoned or sick for long periods of time. They may have mental health problems or their brains weaken. Basically, their response to the world around them decreases.

On the other hand, there are individuals whose astral bodies do not deteriorate. Some of them say that as adults they are the same person they were as a four-year-old. They were just as alert, responsive, vivacious, enthusiastic, receptive, and empathic as a child as they are now. And some of them recall being exactly the same in previous incarnations among human beings. They do not see themselves as changing. They just learn new things. This is a great advantage in that an individual does not have to relearn soul abilities possessed in other lifetimes.

These individuals also have a higher level of energy than

other people, in part because they draw energy directly from nature the way we breathe air into our lungs to sustain our metabolism. They have an extra energy system operating within them. These individuals either were born with the ability or through their love of nature have so joined themselves to one or more elements that they have acquired the astral immortality of elemental beings.

Questions about Incarnated Mermaids

Do children who are incarnated mermaids know they are mermaids, or is there a discovery process involved?

There is no user manual lying next to the crib when they are born that explains that they are not human and then goes on to list the motivations and purposes of the human race. They are here for the human experience. Consequently, as children they start out thinking they are human, but at some point in childhood they figure out on their own that they are not like anyone they have ever met.

In their own realm, the astral, there is no need for a survival instinct or for an ego. This is why, when on Earth, they do not always attach themselves to a social identity; they are not defensive, aggressive, or possessive. Some say they have never had a mean thought in their lives even when someone has intentionally hurt them. Some may adopt social identities for a purpose. Merpeople in human bodies do experience feelings, too! They can feel sadness, anger, and joy like the rest of us. It just doesn't come from a human place of insecurity or a desire for destruction.

In addition, the water element in mermaids animates and makes fully alive whoever they are near. They nurture and they love spontaneously without hesitation and without asking for anything in return. This pure, elemental water in their auras makes them extremely attractive. Because people have never encountered this energy before, it can produce erratic behavior, especially in men. As a consequence, many incarnated mermaids may fabricate a social identity like an actor playing a role to deflect attention and survive among humans.

What are some good career paths for incarnated mermaids?

In general, incarnated merpeople are not usually career oriented, though there are exceptions. Mermaids are usually great in healing roles. They make great therapists, counselors, energy healers, and caretakers. They are very good at grief counseling and have immense success in peacekeeping roles since they are able to empathize with everyone involved. This general guide does not disqualify incarnated merpeople from any career; these are just the ones I see them choosing the most. One of the mermaids I know is an artist and paleontologist!

What are some weaknesses of incarnated mermaids, and how do those weaknesses cause conflict in their lives?

Weaknesses in the human world can be strengths in other parts of the universe. Since they live in the moment, they are not good at planning things out. It helps them to be around people who are very time conscious and success driven.

Mermaids are also very loving and can forgive almost anything. Because of this ability to never become bitter, they can sometimes involve themselves too deeply with abusive people whom they are trying to heal. Mermaids benefit from setting clear boundaries with people and from letting their clients know when they are overstaying their welcome.

Mermaids have auras and personalities that are addicting because they help people feel fully alive. Having rules and making sure that people respect them can prevent problems from arising.

Are you and other incarnated mermaids able to control storms and rain? If so, what is that like for you? Is relating to the sky different from connecting to the ocean?

A few incarnated mermaids have noticed they are able to control weather. Even as children they had this ability. One woman plays in a band that performs outdoors. She has had people come up to her and point out that it never rains while they are playing. Only when they are done does it rain.

The reason incarnated mermaids might have this kind of ability is that as mermaids their souls embody the water element. It may be hard to understand, but they feel united to water in every form, including the water in clouds. For them to say, "It is going to rain now" or "It is going to stop raining" is similar to a human being's consciously recognizing that they are changing their internal feelings and saying, "I am going to calm down now and relax," or, "I am going to recall happy memories."

Just as humans can control their emotions, to control weather is similar for a mermaid. The water in the cloud responds to them because to some extent they have direct power over it. The magnetism in their souls is the same magnetism as in the water in the cloud.

Can starseed souls incarnate as mermaids?

A starseed refers to a soul incarnating here who also has experiences in other star systems, and these beings can incarnate as mermaids. A starseed who is a mermaid is from a water planet. Like a mermaid in our world, her soul is composed of the one element of water, so she acts, feels, loves, and perceives as a mermaid.

However, because the culture of the starseed's home world can be so utterly different from this world, her mind may operate in totally different ways from either human beings or other mermaids. For example, unlike our mermaids, she may have a very sophisticated commitment to pursuing social justice.

If a starseed incarnates on Earth, it is likely the individual's home world may be far more advanced in science and technology than our civilization on Earth. And most likely her society will be quite different from human society. For example, her culture may be far more uniform, integrated, and harmonious.

Consequently, she may bring with her great knowledge and insight. But this knowledge needs to be activated—brought to consciousness—under the right circumstances. Clearly, some are here to help humanity evolve. Similar to the experience mermaids may have as children, they may sense they are from elsewhere. And sometimes they feel so estranged that their primary concern is to return home. Humans often relate easily to starseed mermaids because almost all humans are starseeds themselves. They have incarnated in other places in the universe to advance their spiritual development.

Some men discuss interactions with mermaids as being like cocaine and say that they suffer physical withdrawal symptoms when leaving the mermaid's presence. Can you say why that is?

An incarnated mermaid embodies the water element. Water is receptive, yielding, giving, nurturing, soothing, purifying, and healing. It is ever changing, adapting itself to whatever environment it enters. Place that vibration in a woman's personality and she is extremely vivacious and focused 100 percent on whoever she is with. Without realizing it, she is molding herself to another in such a way as to make that person feel whole and complete.

But she is doing far more with her energy. She can make you feel as if you went rafting down the Colorado River or spent a month camping out in the wilderness. You feel out in nature in her presence without having to go out into nature. You feel free of human time and recharge by being around her.

Now, most people do not notice that she is causing them to feel larger than life, refreshed, and vitalized. Having never witnessed this before, they do not have the words to describe it. But a person's body senses and responds to it. So when you move away from her, say about forty feet, her aura is no longer supplying you with that energy. In returning to what is normal for yourself, you may instead feel half dead without the faintest clue as to why this is.

You can sometimes observe the most rational, stable, and responsible male beginning to panic and have an anxiety attack with the onset of physical withdrawal symptoms when he leaves the presence of one of these women. I have observed this occurring with boyfriends of mermaids I know a number of times.

In a personal relationship with an incarnated mermaid, how might her mermaid love differ from romantic love?

In romantic love, there is an expectation that each partner needs the other. A mermaid, by contrast, does not need another person's love to feel complete or to fill in for something missing from her life. She already feels complete.

Merwomen, then, do not understand attachment. Water has no attachment to the previous moment. It continuously flows, giving all of itself to whatever situation it enters.

Sometimes a male will say with anger to a woman who is a mermaid, "There is nothing to bind us together. I feel as if you don't need me."

One merwoman said, "On occasion, I will pretend that I need my partner for something. For example, I say to him,

'Can you help me with my finances?' And he lights up and becomes enthusiastic because finally I am asking for his help and advice. All the same, I am not comfortable doing this even though it makes him feel good. I am not being truthful when I pretend that I am dependent even in a minor way."

As in the above example, one remedy is for the merwoman to let the guy know how special he is to her and to point out how much she appreciates it whenever he does something for her. However blissful and loving a man's experience with a merwoman is, he will inevitably feel that the relationship is not real unless he senses that she needs him. This can apply to human women in relationships with mermen, too.

A mermaid has to come at least halfway in order to have a relationship. Part of that process is learning to say to the man, "I need you to do this for me. That will make me happy." For many men, words like that are like a tractor beam. They lay hold of him and make him feel connected. Mermaids do not always choose to have relationships with men. Incarnated mermaids can be lesbians, asexuals, autosexuals, and even aromantics just to list a few options. They can be monogamous or polyamorous depending on their personal preferences. The advice I give to mermaids seeking relationships with human men are not meant to displace any other kind of earthly relationships—it is just the most common configuration I have interacted with.

An Answer for a Human
Who Wants to Be a Mermaid

What are some ways that I can share my passion for mermaids to make a difference?

If you are someone who wants to help bring awareness to the existence of mermaids, you can write about them, create artwork, become a speaker on behalf of our planet's water systems, or create discussion groups that teach people about how to develop empathy. Careers in environmental science and natural history are extremely relevant since they are deeply connected to nature and its conservation. Many people are choosing to focus on the environment to protect and preserve nature. You may find the next two chapters especially useful.

As you continue building relationships in the mermaid realm, you may find the answers to questions you did not even know you had. The mermaid realm has many mysteries and gifts to offer, and our exploration of them is something that we can expand on for an entire lifetime.

※

These are just a few questions I have received over the years from people interested in mermaids and their experiences. The exciting part about asking new questions is knowing that you are furthering mermaid research! Sometimes when I receive an inquiry, I have to ask the person who came up with the question to give me time to ask the mermaids or dream with them. Experiencing life here on Earth is a giant discovery process as we make contact with these incredible beings and integrate forgotten parts of ourselves.

CHAPTER 11

How to Become a Mermaid

Everywhere I go I see the evidence of humanity's interest in mermaids. Stores have begun selling more mermaid merchandise. There are mermaid makeup tutorials, mermaid cosplays, and more and more questions being asked about mermaids in forums on the internet. Being able to experience the awakening of humanity to the existence of mermaids is an honor and a privilege for me. Even though we still have a lot to learn, we are well on our way to joining the human and mermaid worlds.

It is true that few mermaids incarnate on Earth from the astral realm. When they do, they live far away from each other, and they do not come back to Earth very often. However, living as a mermaid is not an exclusive club that is reserved for "special" people or those who are "born a certain way." A well-kept secret is that anyone can become a mermaid. It can take time to develop water in one's energy field and to learn to perceive as mermaids do, but it is possible, and it is happening in our world right now.

At this point, I would like to give my readers something that I searched for fervently while I was growing up: that is, how to become a mermaid or how to recognize whether you are one if you already feel as if you are. This is not a list of characteristics meant to discourage people who do not fit them exactly. This is just a set of traits that mermaids usually possess. We can all learn to make these traits part of ourselves, even if we do not believe in the existence of mermaids.

The important thing is to impact our world positively and become the best that we can be. With this in mind, I share a few steps here that may help you clearly understand what to focus on during your mermaid journey.

1. Mermaids teach us that we can love unconditionally and learn to accept everyone we encounter as a beautiful expression of the universe.

Exercise: Take a few moments every day when you can devote all of your energy to feeling deep love and appreciation for everyone and everything in this world (and the universe). Ponder what it means to forgive yourself and others for not being perfect all the time and understand that we are all on this planet to advance our consciousness. Everyone is always unconditionally loved and supported by the universe. We are all equal, are worthy of love, and have a story that is worth being told. Mermaids intuitively know this, and they have no favoritism when it comes to who and how they love.

2. Mermaids are masters of empathy and understanding.

Exercise: Practice putting yourself into other people's shoes. The world is flooded with warlike mentalities, anger, and unresolved pain. Planet Earth needs people who are rooted in compassion and who know how to find peaceful solutions to conflicts. Having empathy and being able to understand why someone is doing what they are doing is a priceless skill and is necessary if we are going to evolve without destroying our planet.

Having empathy is not just limited to feeling it for people. We can have empathy for everything: flowers, trees, plants, animals, ecosystems, and ourselves. Mermaids know that everything has some piece of the universal spirit inside it—every mushroom and stone is an expression of life in its own way. Learning to perceive everything around us as sentient and alive will work wonders as we begin to see what mermaids see and feel what they feel.

3. Mermaids are passionate about nature and the environment because it is part of them and an important part of the universal expression of life.

Exercise: Become involved in the healing of this planet. It is no secret that our oceans are horribly polluted, that the coral reefs are being bleached and killed, and that we could potentially see fishless oceans by 2050. Make changes to practices in your life that can be harmful to the environment. Look into using less plastic, recycling, and trying "meatless Mondays."

Every small change you make is saving the planet and protecting its water and ecosystems. Be involved in keeping your community and natural locations clean. Change can be as simple as starting to pick up trash when you see it lying in the grass or on your local beach. You may eventually feel the mermaids guiding you to certain areas that are desperately in need of cleanup.

4. Mermaids realize that everything is interconnected. This concept goes hand in hand with empathy and caring for the environment.

Exercise: Examine the interconnectedness of all life. Do you feel that you are better than forest animals or that sharks are superior to schooling fish? In our world we think of certain creatures as superior to others based on who eats whom and who seems to have more influence in the world. Mermaids do not think like this because they possess ecological consciousness. This means that they understand that every speck in existence has an important role to play in the evolution of the universe.

5. Mermaids cultivate the water element in their auras and anchor the Earth's energy.

Exercise: Learn to make water part of yourself and adopt it as a permanent part of your energy field. Spend time in water, and meditate with it as often as you can. Earth is full of a lot of out-of-balance fire energy (the energy that usually destroys and the energy that causes wars). We need people who are grounding the water element and anchoring it here on this planet. Developing empathy and love for everyone here is evidence that you are becoming adept with the water element. Fundamentally, mermaids are beings who have water in their auras. When you make water part of yourself, they recognize you as one of their own.

⋇

Grounding the spiritual mermaid experience in the physical world is essential to developing a stronger connection to the mer-realm on earth. Making sure that kindness and love are informing our actions is even more important than meditating on the water element all day. The general guidelines presented here are bread crumbs you can follow as you develop your own personal relationships within the mer-realm and discover how your unique vibration can positively impact the mermaid experience on Earth. There are many paths to be trod when it comes to integrating the spiritual water element in the third dimension, and the merfolk are willing to share their secrets to mastery as long as we come to them from a place of virtue and equity.

CHAPTER 12

How to Make a Difference as a Mermaid

Without a practical application in our world, there is little point in studying mermaids or becoming like them. But I believe that developing the qualities of mermaids does have practical applications: it opens doors to changing the current state of this planet without having to have a college degree, money, or the ability to travel. Education is important, and money has its purposes in our world, but the point is that anyone can become like mermaids regardless of where they are at in life. So why are mermaids here on Earth, and how does their presence make anything better?

Our oceans are desperately in need of cleanup, and doing hands-on work to save them is extremely important. However, ocean cleanup is not going to be a total fix, since the people who are polluting the planet continue to show disrespect for the ocean and the life in it. How do we solve this? This is where a mermaid approach comes in. It is a very different method from the way humans normally handle things because it is completely psychic in nature.

Franz Bardon was a famous occultist and a teacher for an advanced magical system called Hermetics. Hermetics teaches students how to interconnect the worlds of nature, spirit, and humanity. Bardon's material will help anyone to train their mind to be able to perceive feelings and vibrations in the astral realm.

One of the many benefits that can come from learning how to meditate with Hermetics is that the individual can learn to set their ego aside so that messages from the astral realm come through clearly. In Bardon's book *Initiation into Hermetics,* students lay the groundwork and foundation for all of their psychic endeavors. Meditations and mental training exercises help the student develop mental clarity, control of thoughts, and sensory awareness. All of these things are important because if your mind is constantly filling up with thoughts, a mermaid's message or feeling will not be able to get through to you. Sensory training is also important so that you will be able to perceive when energy fluctuates and when an elemental is communicating with you. Other skills you will learn include developing clairsentience (feeling), discernment, and accumulating the water element in your body. Think of Hermetics, meditations in general, and mental exercises as the ladder that you climb to become a master of yourself and a master of your chosen element. Even if you do not want to become a lifelong student of the Hermetic system, the mental training exercises and meditations will help you develop the skills necessary to expand your empathy beyond the realm of humans. And this will help you to communicate with more forms of spirit than you can currently imagine.

Deeper into the Hermetic training system, you will find what are known as cosmic letters or cosmic numbers. Each number or letter basically represents a signature vibration that is like a phone number for contacting certain elemental realms and elementals themselves. The letters or numbers are vibrations that are accessed through visualization, sound, concentration on imagery and feeling, and oneness with the element that it represents.

For example, to meditate on the cosmic letter *M,* you imagine a blue-green color, the musical note of D, and the sensation of cold water, and you focus on your abdomen where the water element naturally resides. (Each body organ is associated with a different element. Focusing on the body part that pertains to the element you are wishing to use will help you concentrate the feeling in a physical sense and then project it into the astral realm.)

The cosmic letter *M* enables a student to master all of the water element that exists in the universe. If you want to be able to sense every emotion that exists within man and within the mermaid realm, I would strongly suggest you spend a significant amount of time with the letter *M.*

The cosmic alphabet is not simply our phonetic alphabet used for physical communication. Each letter represents mastery over a certain element and the specific talents within that elemental realm. Each letter has benefits for the material, astral, and mental planes.

On the mental plane, students who become adept with the cosmic letter *M* can become masters of their feelings and can become aware of dimensions of emotion that humans do not even know about. These emotions and sensations have great power because they can represent levels of love that dissolve all hatred, all wars, and all turbulence within the human mind.

What magicians, students, and humans achieve through the cosmic letters and Hermetic system is what mermaids experience all the time. Mermaids already have complete mastery over their element to the point where they can sense every molecule of water in the ocean. What we use as a system is their natural way of life and perception. What follows is a specific example of what someone can do with cosmic letters in the Hermetic system and how meditation with a cosmic letter can affect planet Earth.

~~~~~~

🐟 Hermetic Meditation on the Letter W

This meditation is an example of something I do on a daily basis to create more harmony and understanding among world leaders. This is a meditation on the cosmic letter W, and I almost always have several astral mermaids join me. Since the cosmic letter W is united with the element of water, it works the same for both mermaids and humans.

Find a quiet space to sit in the dark. (I usually do this meditation at night with all of the lights out so that I can be free of distractions.) If you would like to, close your eyes. Notice what you feel. Perhaps you will visualize a color (in this space I see lilac as the color of water and imagine it as a waterfall terminating in a pool). The color you see will be so beautiful that you may also feel that you never have to do anything or be anything other than what you are being right now.

You may feel a sense of satisfaction in your abdomen and stomach, as if you will never be hungry again, as if all of your purposes are complete, and as if everything you can be is available to you right now. In this moment you are the best version of yourself. There is nothing to prove, validate, or succeed at right now. There is only now.

Feel your physical body become immersed in cold, lilac-colored water. Drops of this water roll down your chest, down your thighs, and all the way to your feet. Become one with this water. Unite with this water in a feeling of euphoria and bliss.

As this lilac water, turn your attention to some world leader, such as the president of the United States. Imagine yourself entering this person's stomach and abdomen. Allow your color, your feeling, and your watery essence to slowly become part of this person in this moment.

Influence this person to begin to feel as you feel and perceive as you perceive. Feel the water in nature responding to your visualization. Let its presence surround you both with sweet sensation. As this happens, the person you are influencing will align with the cosmos. The cosmic love of the universe will enter the field through the water that surrounds you. You may feel the person's mood and even consciousness shift. At this point, the person may begin to hear the spirit guides and highly evolved beings in the universe.

When you sense your mission is complete and the person has received your healing energy, gently pull back your consciousness from this other person's. Begin to wriggle your fingers and toes slowly and come back to your physical self.

Over the past several years, I have attempted to influence the president into feeling that there is nothing to be other than all that we are. We do not need to enforce patriarchal beliefs or formulate plans that keep certain groups of people oppressed. This feeling is so good and total that we want everyone on our planet to feel this way.

When the president would align with the part of himself that is always one with God, light, or the universal source, I could feel all tiredness leave his body and mind. This is when he would begin to hear the spirit guides and highly evolved beings in the universe. He heard them speaking to his consciousness and affirming his worth and connection to them.

For these few minutes, the cosmic love that infiltrates the universe would enter the water I had become, and it would become part of the president on a physical, mental, and astral levels. His aura would begin to change to reflect this union. When I sensed that he had received his daily dose of healing energy for one day, I pulled my consciousness away from his energy field, leaving the lilac water behind—still part of him. When I would begin coming back into my body, the feeling of bliss would not fade.

I could see with my mind's eye that he was in a more relaxed state. For one more day, he would not feel the need to respond angrily to others' critical remarks. He shared his good mood with his family and met a few needs that he had not previously cared about. Since he is a figure that attracts a great amount of attention, many people's consciousnesses are connected to him. His positive feeling would go out to them and affect them, too. The water in him subtly spoke to the water inside everyone who felt connected to his presidency. I like to call this the ripple effect.

The implications for the practice shared above are immense—ending wars, healing people from a distance, tele-pathically communicating loving thoughts to world leaders, and using the water element to distribute resources through-out the planet. This meditation can completely change the dynamics that are currently wreaking havoc on society and the environment.

If a world leader is frustrated because he or she has no ability to connect to a partner or has insufficient empathy to have a satisfying love life, the leader can act out and cause wars to help affirm his or her personal power and sense of self. As simplistic as it may seem, this happens all the time. What if there were a group of people on Earth who gained mastery over feelings of peace and who were able to enter the dreams of others to create peace and satisfaction within them? What if they were able to sense what was in people's hearts and place a permanent feeling of godlike love within them?

Performing energy work for other humans is not the only practical way mermaids influence the planet. Skill in working with the water element can also aid in ocean cleanup, a passion shared by all merpeople. Through a highly evolved feeling that is only learned from the mermaid realm, humans and mermaids can speed up the vibration of water. This can cause the water to dissolve and "zap" particles of pollution that permeate our ocean.

There are some pieces of trash in the ocean that are nearly impossible to notice with our physical eyes, and they are even harder to access. Only a select few have been able to travel to the great depths of the ocean floor and remain there for any amount of time. Because of this, teaching water to heal itself is extremely important to mermaids. They are willing to teach this skill to anyone who has the basic ability to communicate with them and direct the water element's energy.

What I have shared with you is not an actual lesson in Hermetics or empathy. It is just an example of all of the possibilities that are available to humans who choose to master themselves and use their connection to the mermaid realm to change the world. Psychic solutions are meant to work hand in hand with physical actions and activism. Right now physical efforts to clean up the ocean have the greatest impact. I am still learning the above skill myself and am not always consistent with it. These solutions employed together are ethical and productive, since they heal the source of strife and anger inside ourselves instead of just addressing symptoms of this distress.

The mermaid queen Isaphil says it this way:

> *I have feelings that are so sweet that if a few aspired to share them with humanity, they would heal every hurt in the span of a heartbeat.*

CHAPTER 13

A Word of Caution

Without the water element, spiritual and physical eco-systems are thrown out of balance. For example, the fire element is a necessary and powerful force for humans and planet Earth when it is kept in balance. However, when fire exists without water, spiritual asymmetry manifests as rage, cruelty, hazing, domination, narcissism, and destruction of important ecosystems. This ultimately results in the collapse of physical, mental, emotional, and spiritual infrastructure.

Humans are currently exploring a variety of realities through their media, thoughts, and dreams. The video game *Cyberpunk 2077* takes players to a world where greed, corporate war, and a lack of respect for natural resources have completely destroyed the planet as we know it. Crime and poverty have overrun extant cities, and human beings physically augment themselves to become weaponized. Deforestation has caused acid rain and severe dust storms in this virtual reality and has resulted in the devastation of the natural landscape. This is a world without a spiritually and physically healthy water element.

Cyberpunk 2077 is just one example of an alternate reality humans are exploring through media outlets that provide an eerie parallel to current events. The coronavirus pandemic, oppression and abuse of minorities and people of color, riots, bushfires, earthquakes, and locust swarms in Africa are all red flags pointing toward a world where humans are ruled by fear and greed. We must heed this warning before it is too late. Planet Earth is sending desperate messages to humanity, but not everyone is in the receptive, watery state that empowers them to properly interpret the messages and make course corrections.

The time has come for humans to become all that they can be and to fully embrace the golden age. The golden age means we create "heaven on Earth" and make every moment so beautiful that there is nowhere else we would rather be. This is simple but difficult, considering we must rewrite our own programming and shift into a loving and empathic state while so many people in the world bombard us with fear, hate, and destructive tendencies.

Donning mermaid tails, owning pet fish, and supporting mermaid merchandise companies is fun and makes life beautiful, but it is not enough. We must become what a mermaid (or merman) is. We must choose love, empathy, and "now" consciousness to be in alignment with a reality where Earth succeeds. We must take physical action when and where we can. Every decision we make can be conscious and rooted in a desire for the good of all. Separatism, colonialism, and supremacy have no footholds in the mermaid realm, where everyone is nurtured, safe, and provided for. There is no fear or lack because everyone has what they need, and everyone is loved.

Although planet Earth is not the only realm where the mermaid kingdom exists, it is the giant spaceship that serves as the physical incubator for humans, animals, and plants as they evolve. Humans have already invested thousands of years into their own evolution, spiritually and otherwise. Starting over would have devastating consequences for future races, species, and consciousness. No one wants to begin such a massive undertaking from scratch.

Humans stand on the brink of the sixth extinction. Changes are occurring in the atmosphere as well as in the ocean and on land: from differences in the North Atlantic current, to sea acidity, to the oceans' ability to absorb heat, to loss of forests and native fauna. What can we do?

Mermaids instinctively nurture everything around them, and now humans must do the same. Every spiritual journey must be juxtaposed with physical action to anchor the results into our domain. Participating in ocean cleanup projects, educating fellow humans about how daily choices can influence animals and ecosystems, and diligently engaging with the hearts and minds of world leaders is imperative for Earth to be able to heal.

Some humans are actually mermaids in human bodies. Other humans simply have unique gifts that grant them special connections to the mermaid realm. But these connections are possible for anyone no matter who they are, where they live, or what they look like. Initiates, masters, spiritual seekers, and even people who just love water have asked how humans can bring the heart of the mermaid realm to our world.

Mermaids answered our call and have given us gentle

instructions and lessons we can integrate inside ourselves. We have all the tools we need to feel part of oceans, lakes, rivers, ponds, and streams that restore Earth's equilibrium. Do this by loving nature. We must hold nature in our hearts and make the nurturing, healing qualities of water part of ourselves.

The reality we will experience in the next few years will be determined by the state of being we embody and the choices we make now. Wherever we are, we can act as representatives and ambassadors for the mermaid realm and become living, breathing sanctuaries for the water element before it disappears from our world.

Additional Mermaid Resources

During my teenage years, I searched for resources that would help me and others become more connected to the mermaid realm. Ultimately the answer is inside ourselves, and it has a lot to do with how much time we spend developing our connection to the water element. However, there are some amazing resources in our world that can help us have an easier, more enjoyable mermaid experience, and I would like to share some of my favorites.

Books

Oceana: Our Endangered Oceans and What We Can Do to Save Them by **Ted Danson** is a book that everyone who is interested in saving the oceans will want to read. Danson explains the problems that our oceans are facing due to human behavior and tells what we can do to save the water on our planet and the life it contains.

What a Fish Knows: The Inner Lives of Our Underwater Cousins by **Jonathan Balcombe** is one of my favorite books—and this is coming from a bookworm who reads several books per week! This book brings readers to a greater understanding of how fish experience the world and poses that they are spiritual, valuable beings like ourselves. It is a wonderful prerequisite for people who would like to develop friendships with fish.

The Practice of Magical Evocation by **Franz Bardon** is an in-depth study of elemental spirits along with spirits of many other zones or spheres. Bardon describes the skills and areas of specialization of hundreds of these spirits.

The Key to the True Kabbalah by **Franz Bardon** will guide students to vibrational gateways that alter the course of humanity.

Initiation into Hermetics by **Franz Bardon** will help students form the mental and psychic foundation skills necessary to communicate with elemental realms.

Franz Bardon is a master in the Western system of Hermetics. He died in the 1950s. Bardon emphasizes in his first book, *Initiation into Hermetics,* a careful, systematic, and step-by-step guide to training. The idea is to develop the student's body, soul, and mind so they are in complete harmony at all times during the course of study.

One of the unique features of his system is his focus on the four elements of earth, air, fire, and water as energies and vibrations to master in ourselves. The earth element leads to being practical, productive, and effective in the physical world. Those who possess these qualities are said to be down to earth. The water element develops sensitivity, empathy, love, and nurturing qualities. The air element develops artistic sensitivity, detachment, openness of mind, playfulness, cheerfulness, and an appreciation of freedom. The fire element develops resolution, willpower, determination, and commitment to accomplishing your goals in specific time frames. Through the exercises with the elements, the student takes what is weak in his soul and makes it stronger. He takes what is negative or passive and makes it positive and active.

At the end of *Initiation into Hermetics,* after a massive amount of training in the basics, Bardon guides the student to enter the realms of the four elemental beings on the astral plane. There the student makes direct contact with mermaids, sylphs, gnomes, and salamanders. Insisting on direct, first-hand, and personal experience, the student is to learn all he or she can from these beings. In effect, the student is making these magical realms a second home.

Franz Bardon's students are in the process of creating archives and online classes and publishing a great many books on their own experiences with Bardon's system. Over the course of time, elemental beings will come to be treated not as something dangerous that requires massive preparation to interact with. They will dwell among us. We will be able to meet incarnated elementals and talk to them face-to-face without there being a threat to our personal identity or our "magical authority." At that point, we will have created a genuine spiritual community.

Some of Bardon's current students who publish their own material are Rawn Clark, Martin Faulks, Ray del Sole,

Virgil, William Mistele, Julia Griffin, Emil Stejnar, Nenad Djordjevic-Talerman, Kadiliya Aili, and Andre Consciencia.

Undines: Lessons from the Realm of the Water Spirits **by William Mistele** is a book that specifically talks about mermaids. William is a dear friend of mine who has studied incarnated mermaid women for the past several decades. His books provide information on how to develop empathy and how to make contact with the mermaid people, and they go into detail about the auras and personalities of astral mermaids. *Undines* is the book that I always wished that I had while growing up.

See also his books *The Four Elements* and *Mermaid Tales; Mermaids, Sylphs, Gnomes, and Salamanders* as well as his upcoming book, *Ten Rules for Spiritual Beginners*.

Mistele calls himself a spiritual anthropologist. As such, his interest is in extracting and integrating the universal contributions from all spiritual and wisdom traditions. Spiritual anthropology asks age-old questions: What is it to be a human being? What is human nature? What is it to be and to feel fully alive?

Mistele also calls himself a bardic magician and uses the mediums of poetry, short stories, novels, and screenplays to present modern fairy tales and mythology. This genre asks questions such as: How do we discover the divinity within ourselves? And how do we apply our divine powers so they are effective in transforming the world in which we live?

For Mistele, magic is a study of how to make the best choices in life. For those who are up for it, the study of magic accelerates your learning process and grants you greater depth and variety of life experiences. After forty-five years of studying Bardon's system, Mistele has gone on to apply his magical skills to establishing justice between nations.

See his videos on YouTube in which he, Avaah Blackwell, and Aaron interview a number of mermaids and mermen described in Franz Bardon's book, *The Practice of Magical Evocation*. He also has a large number of videos, including some he has made with me, on his Facebook page (under his name, William R. Mistele).

Documentaries

Mission of Mermaids (directed by Susan Rockefeller, 2012) is a beautiful short film about ocean activism and the role of mermaids in society. Available on Vimeo.

A Sea Change (directed by Barbara Ettinger, 2009) is a documentary about ocean acidification and how the oceans are in need of an immediate change in human behavior. For those wanting to expand their knowledge of how to save the oceans, this documentary is worth your time. Available on Vimeo.

Where to Purchase Mermaid Tails

Dressing up like a mermaid is becoming an increasingly sought-after activity for people who want to be mermaids. There are many amazing tailmakers in our world, but I will list a couple of my favorites here. All have a web presence, so be sure to check out their websites. You can also learn how to make your own tails and create your own designs.

Finfolk Productions custom mermaid tails are absolutely amazing. They are pricey but worth every penny. They sell other mermaid merchandise, too, and I enjoy looking through their online shop.

The Mertailor, also known as Eric Ducharme, is one of my favorite tailmakers because he has so much variety and makes tails for all age groups. He has affordable tails, eco-friendly tails, and custom tails that can be used by the professional mermaid.

The Mermaid Community

I adore **AquaMermaid's YouTube channel** because she offers an all-encompassing crash course in mermaiding. Whether you want to be professional or just swim in a tail for fun, AquaMermaid can help educate you and direct you to wonderful resources in that world.

The MerNetwork is an online community of people who love to make, swim in, and perform in mermaid tails. This is a place where you can discuss all of your mermaiding needs and receive advice from veteran tailmakers and swimmers.

Music

Sirens of the Sea **by Oceanlab** is one of my favorite musical albums. A lot of albums about mermaids or mermaid energy are just instrumental (which is beautiful, too), but I love this album because the lyrics are powerful and motivating. My favorite song is "Miracle." I listen to it before starting any conservation projects and am unstoppable for the rest of the day. The album is available on iTunes, Spotify, and Amazon.

Websites for Merfolk Information

William Mistele's undine homepage is a wonderful resource for extra information about mermaids. It is part of a larger website that discusses Hermetic wisdom, other types of elementals, and provides meditations. His website includes essays, stories, and biographies about mermaids.

Save the Mermaids is a mermaid blog devoted to the conservation of our oceans and watery ecosystems. I love their Mermaid Challenge program and appreciate how they educate humans about ocean pollution.

Index

113